Transformational Steps for Ordinary People

A Christ-Centered Twelve Step Study Guide

by
Teresa McBean

A publication of the
National Association
for Christian Recovery

ISBN-13: 978-1495237805
ISBN-10: 149523780X

Cover art by Rachel Hartshorn of Hartshorn Books

Copyright © 2014
National Association for Christian Recovery
561 Southlake Blvd.
Richmond, VA 23235
Web: www.nacr.org
Voice: 800.908.2377

Table of Contents

Prayer for Serenity

Across various disciplines of study on addiction, there is a general consensus that addiction includes a component of spiritual malaise. Depending on the lens of expertise through which one views addiction, the nature of the affliction and the emphasis on the spiritual malady varies. But anyone who has struggled personally with addiction gets this: there comes a moment when we realize that we cannot change without rescue. All our attempts to manage our lives have crashed and burned. Those who choose to work the 12 steps are not asked to sort out all this spirituality stuff before starting the journey, but it does help to find a way to acknowledge the need for help from God. This prayer has been helpful to many in this process. If the spiritual part of this program concerns you, maybe start here—pray this prayer daily.

God, grant me the serenity to accept the things I cannot change,

the courage to change the things I can,

and the wisdom to know the difference.

Living one day at a time, enjoying one moment at a time;

accepting hardship as a pathway to peace;

taking, as Jesus did, this sinful world as it is;

not as I would have it;

trusting that You will make all things right

if I surrender to your will;

so that I may be reasonably happy in this life

and supremely happy with You

forever in the next.

Amen

INTRODUCTION

The twelve steps are a remarkable spiritual tool which many users speak about as "life transforming." I know some folks think the twelve steps are only for people with addiction issues. As a pastor working within the context of a recovery ministry and as Executive Director of the National Association for Christian Recovery, my experience has taught me that these steps have transformative potential for anyone willing to work them—not just addicts and their beloved co-dependents.

All of us, every single person I've ever known, desperately needs transformation. Some of us are aware of our need for change, and some are not. Some of us become willing to admit our need for rescue. Sadly, some remain stubbornly resistant. All of us, whether we acknowledge it or not, struggle with living out God's promise to restore and his exhortation to embrace the work of faithful living (See James 1 and Romans 12). If we think for just a few seconds about the scripture's descriptions of faithful living in contrast to our own personal experiences with selfishness, abuse, neglect and cruelty, it's not a stretch for us to admit that we need help learning how to live faithfully. I myself know it's difficult to find examples of faithfulness to follow. Yet I dare to dream that if I work these steps, I might learn a new way to live…and perhaps have an experience I can share with others in need of a path out of bondage and into the light of recovery. Here's one biblical description of the problem we face:

"There's nobody living right, not even one, nobody who knows the score, nobody alert for God. They've all taken the wrong turn; they've all wandered down blind alleys. No one's living right; I can't find a single one. Their throats are gaping graves, their tongues slick as mud slides. Every word they speak is tinged with poison. They open their mouths and pollute the air. They race for the honor of sinner-of-the-year, litter the land with heartbreak and ruin, don't know the first thing about living with others. They never give God the time of day. This makes it clear, doesn't it, that whatever is written in these Scriptures is not what God says about others but to us to whom these Scriptures were addressed in the first place! And it's clear enough, isn't it, that we're sinners, every one of us, in the same sinking boat with everybody else?" (Romans 3:10-20 *The Message*)

Alcoholics Anonymous (AA) began on June 10, 1935 with two men in search of transformation. A part of that transformation process included finding their freedom from alcoholism. In the 1920s and 1930s, a

Lutheran pastor, Dr. Frank N. D. Buchman, led a community of believers called the Oxford Group. Evangelistic in their mission and passionate about rekindling faith in a church grown cold, they declared the group an "organism" instead of an "organization." The group's teachings rested on the following principles:

1. Human beings are sinners.
2. Human beings can be changed.
3. Confession is a prerequisite to change.
4. The changed soul has direct access to God.
5. The age of miracles has returned.
6. Those who have been changed are to change others.[1]

The co-founders of AA studied with the Oxford Group, and one of those founders, Bill Wilson, later recalled:

"It was from Sam Shoemaker [an American clergyman with the Oxford Group] that we absorbed most of the Twelve Steps of Alcoholics Anonymous, steps that express the heart of AA's way of life. The early AA got its ideas of self-examination, acknowledgement of character defects, restitution of harm done and working with others straight from the Oxford Group and directly from Sam Shoemaker, their former leader in America, and from nowhere else."[2]

I believe these men were on to something. They studied God's word and used it to order their lives. They also took the time to study their lives—taking fearless personal moral inventories—and asked God to change anything in them that was not in keeping with the character of a godly man or woman. They dared to believe that they could live transformed lives for the glory of God—and guess what? Their belief did not disappoint. Their faith was properly placed in the one who saves and transforms!

It is my prayer that these study guides will be tools God uses to bless you with the same kind of miraculous healing power that others have experienced using these twelve steps. The National Association for Christian Recovery (NACR) joins with the Oxford Group of old and their buddies at AA in believing that all things are possible. You too can become the person God intended you to become! May these guides be one instrument God uses, and may his name be glorified in the process.

Suggestions for using these materials

These materials are not intended for eager beavers interested in racing through them so that the participant can say, "Hey, been there, worked those steps!" There are plenty of fabulous resources on the market about the steps, the Big Book of AA being the most notable and worthy resource that comes to my mind. However, I felt something was missing for me. I wanted a resource that gave me lots of scriptures to turn to and read as I worked my program of recovery. In my own work, I found myself filling journals and messing up my Bible margins with notes about how I experienced my step work and Bible reading as concurrent and mutually supportive resources. I assumed that there might be others out in the world interested in the same kind of process. I recommend that instead of taking all these scriptures available with each question, choose selectively and read carefully rather than rushing through and using them all at once (although that's a fine option too). I would encourage using the steps as a daily practice.

Secondly, I cannot urge participants strongly and loudly enough *not* to study in isolation. The value of a group is priceless. I hope you'll gather a group of your friends and study through each one of the twelve steps. Inevitably, the inclination to isolate and hide will tempt us to grab this workbook, take it home and study by ourselves. (Can't we just figure this stuff out and get on with life without bringing other people into our problems? Experienced steppers would answer that question: "No!") Anytime we get exposure to God's word, that's a great thing. But to really grow, we need community.

Thirdly, I encourage you to find a spiritual mentor/sponsor who has experience with these steps and ask them to act as an accountability partner.

And, finally, I encourage you to supplement this work with other readings (See the recommendations at the back of this study guide). Go online (www.nacr.org), attend meetings, find and show up regularly at places of worship that are recovery focused or at least recovery friendly. In other words, this material comes with a warning label: don't try to do this alone! Enjoy! Blessings.

Step 1

*We admitted that we were powerless over
our dependencies—that our lives had become
unmanageable.*

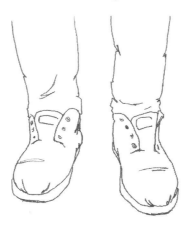

Introduction

Over twenty years ago, my brother acknowledged his addictions and entered a treatment facility in Atlanta, GA, after spending Christmas with our entire family at a fancy resort in Florida. It became apparent to him that his using was out of control. Neither he nor any other human can fully explain why, upon returning from our Christmas trip and trying unsuccessfully to kill himself with his drug of choice, he called my brother and said, "I need help." I personally think it was a God thing. The first step he took toward a recovered life was one of acknowledgement—I need help; my life is unmanageable.

One of my brother's first requests in treatment was for our family to get help along with him. I decided that the way I could support his recovery was by entering the meeting rooms myself, joining him in the 12-step work. My focus was on my codependency issues, but it soon became apparent to me that my battle with an eating disorder wasn't so different from my brother's obsession with cocaine. Upon realizing this, I also began to work the steps as a means to treat my own compulsivity. My brother wasn't the only one in our family with dependencies, powerlessness, and unmanageability issues; it was just that his out-of-control using was more obvious. My brother and I agree that our experiences with recovery are remarkably similar. Both of us believe that a large part of our collective work has focused around understanding self-deception and learning how to move beyond our denial. Denial is an amazing thing. It is exceedingly damaging and can be as fatal as too much crack. Our family's recovery is not unique—in fact, it's more common than we'd like to admit.

I have discovered, however, that the value of the 12-step work extends far beyond the assistance it provided my family in recovery. My mother is currently coming to grips with a health diagnosis that no one wants to receive. My heartbreak over this dread disease and its ensnarement of my mom has been more over the denial around it than the actual disease itself (and that's saying a LOT because the disease is a nasty one). My family has struggled, as I understand is very common in situations like this, to acknowledge my mother's decline. Failure on our part to admit the reality of our situation has led to some consequences—medication messes, driving and getting lost, misunderstandings about why mom never calls us anymore, hurt feelings, and even the occasional temper tantrum. We as a family have not been able to share our burdens openly because we have been trying to keep the obvious a secret. This has isolated us, made the burden heavier, and actually put our beloved mother and all other Atlanta drivers at risk. We're moving beyond denial into the truth, but it isn't easy. My experience working the 12 steps and applying these principles in all my affairs is helping me recover my life during this tragedy, just as they did so many years ago when I woke up to my codependent and eating disordered ways.

Welcome to step 1. Maybe you, like our family, are struggling with powerlessness and unmanageability that is not directly related to substance abuse. That's okay. We have found that these steps, when we work them, help us recover our lives from many struggles. It works if you work it. Now let's get started!

In this workbook we are going to look, in detail, at the meaning of each step. After we overview the step, we will have questions and scriptures to read and consider. I highly recommend that participants find a small group and a safe and experienced spiritual mentor (in the program we call that person a "sponsor") to help with this work. An experienced sponsor encourages us and shares his or her own experience, strength, and hope without judging our work or controlling our outcome. I pray that you can find someone to share this journey with. Community seems to be an essential element of recovery work.

Key Terms

Powerless: It's a tough concept, but it doesn't make sense to proceed until this admission is made. I do not have the power to live life well. My life is not working for me. I do not have the power to make decisions and navigate life in a way that is manageable. I have not been able to design a life that results in reasonable happiness and a sense of satisfaction about my current conditions. At the heart of powerlessness is the acknowledgement that I cannot stop doing whatever I'm doing that leads to unmanageability; nor can I maintain the choices that are positive, healing and healthy—in keeping with the deepest desires of my heart. When all my strategies to control myself and others stop working and I cannot find new strategies that do work, I am ready for step 1.

Unmanageable: This is when life is out of control. We may not feel the craziness. But if we had the courage to ask, would those who know us well say our life is unmanageable? I sometimes get angry and withdraw from people who try to tell me that I'm out of control. In the moment of the conversation, I'm more defensive than grateful for their concern and I struggle to see my life from their perspective. Here are some questions I've learned to ask myself as a way to wake up to my life when I fall back into my old codependent, unmanageable ways: Am I forgetful? Do I feel crazy? Do bad things keep happening and I don't know why?

People get confused and think that only addicts have unmanageable lives, but that's not true. Unmanageability can be found in: relationships, eating, finances, religion, work, health—anything that has such a hold on us that we find other areas of our life impacted negatively. Our lives can be orderly. I'm not talking rigid, over-scheduled or inflexible. I am talking calm, peaceful, and just plain good. We were created for a good life. Another clue that life has gotten unmanageable has to do with desire. If we desire to change more than anything, if we have given it our best shot and still nothing changes—then step 1 is a decent next right step.

Dependencies: These are the people, places, and/or things that, if we are brutally honest, we do not think we could live without. They are the things we cling to even when clear evidence indicates that they are harming us and those we love. Dr. Archibald Hart wrote a book (*Healing Life's Hidden Addictions*) in which he proposes that all of us struggle with dependencies. Other authors, including Gerald May, share his perspective. I may not have issues with alcohol or drugs that you buy from your local dealer, but I've got dependency issues.

One summer I was going to be away from home for several weeks in a row because of business commitments. I dreaded the time away from home. I'm not much of a traveler by nature. Simultaneously, and completely unconsciously, I began to obsess over all the times in the next few weeks when I would be forced to drink my morning coffee out of a foam cup. (It turns out that one of my favorite ritualistic dependencies is going down to the kitchen before the sun wakes up, picking a favorite mug and sipping a piping hot cup of coffee in peace and quiet.) My obsession over my loss of my morning routine resulted in me packing several mugs in my luggage. Problem solved? Well, not quite, because the problem really wasn't my morning coffee. My issue was that I was feeling uncomfortable and was asking for one of my dependencies to soothe my frazzled nerves—without actually having to deal with the root issue of my dis-ease. This is what dependencies promise us—a way around our underlying anxieties and secret fears, our unresolved issues and childhood wounds. But dependencies cannot deliver on their promises, and that's one of the principles we'll learn as we walk through these steps.

Denial: Denial is so much more than a river in Egypt! It's that stubborn propensity to see things from a skewed perspective. Here's a fancy definition for denial as it relates to alcoholism:

"Alcoholism is a primary, chronic disease with genetic, psycho-social, and environmental factors influencing its development and manifestations. The disease is often progressive and fatal. It is characterized by continuous or periodic: impaired control over drinking, preoccupation with the drug alcohol, use of alcohol despite adverse consequences, and distortions in thinking, most notably denial…Denial is used here not only in the psychoanalytic sense of a single psychological defense mechanism disavowing the significance of events, but more broadly to include a range of psychological maneuvers designed to reduce awareness of the fact that alcohol use is the cause of an individual's problems rather than a solution to those problems. Denial becomes an integral part of the disease and a major obstacle to recovery." [3]

Admit: In *Addictive Thinking*, Abraham Twerski also talks about denial and self-deception: "I cannot stress enough the importance of realizing that addicts are taken in by their own distorted thinking and that they are its victims. If we fail to understand this, we may feel frustrated or angry in dealing with the addict." [4]

My coffee mug obsession is a dependency and a symbol for me of my denial-prone tendencies. My longing for my morning ritual is somehow easier to obsess over than to acknowledge that my trip will cause me to miss my son's lacrosse game, my daughter's piano recital, and my husband's cuddly presence each night when I turn into bed after a long day. The way we distract ourselves from the "real deal" is harmful in two ways. First, the dependency/compulsion attachment is limiting. And, secondly, the failure to work through our real heart issues means that our growth and maturation process is stunted. (This topic will be developed further as we work through the steps.) For now, the key point is this: denial is a wall of limitation. It keeps us from naming our problem, which ensures that we are not free to find the solution. Admitting our powerlessness is the ticket out. Admitting that we have a problem drags it out of the darkness into God's wonderful light. God is in the business of rescue and recovery, but he's extremely respectful of our right to choose our own path. He won't violate our right not to want his awesome healing power.

Power: The key to the first step is acknowledging our powerlessness. We do not have the power to change ourselves or others. We can't change many of our life circumstances. But there is power available, and we desperately want to have it. Paradox is an amazing thing. In recovery, we learn that until we relinquish the lie that we are powerful, we can never truly experience God's power lived out, in, and through us.

Congratulations! We wouldn't be in this study unless something about our lives was not satisfactory. It takes courage to admit that and even greater courage to show up and admit that to a group of fellow sojourners. At some level we've had to bust through the barrier of denial to show up for this work.

Step 1: Making it Personal

Before we begin: As we work these steps, we may find that certain words, phrases or stories "trigger us" in ways that cause us to feel ashamed or defensive. The first word I want to warn you about is the "s" word—sin. Mention "sin," and my shame is triggered. This reaction stymied my recovery until I learned more about the concept of sin. Instead of thinking of sin as bad behaving, I encourage you to think of sin as "living independently of our higher power." Sin means losing touch with my spirituality, my true purpose for living, and my capacity to live comfortably in community with others.

1) Read Jeremiah 6:14. Are there wounds that you've pretended aren't "that bad?"

2) Read Proverbs 28:13 and 2 Peter 2:19. What failures have you experienced in your life?

3) How have you been feeling lately? Maybe you think your circumstances have caused you to have these feelings. Scripture gives us a renewed way of thinking about our feelings. Read Psalms 6:6-7; 32:3-5; 40:12. After reading the scriptures, what else might be going on that you hadn't considered?

4) Make a list of things going on in your life that are out of control.

5) What are the emotions, actions, and thoughts that keep repeating in your life in unmanageable ways?

6) Read Galatians 5:19-23. Whenever life is out of control, there are probably some things we have or are doing that fill us with guilt. Additionally, some of us are overwhelmed by our shame. Shame is the feeling that leads me to believe that I'm not only doing wrong, but that I am somehow without value. In the work we are starting we'll differentiate between guilt and shame; for today, know that there are natural consequences when we mess up. But what might trip us up is

our unacknowledged shame. We'll work on this. We'll find a way to deal restoratively with our guilt, and I suspect that the work itself will be potentially healing for our unhealthy shame attacks.

How have your best efforts worked for you? What specifically are you ready to admit is unmanageable about your life?

7) Read 2 Corinthians 1:8-9 and Jeremiah 29:11-12. I know looking at failures and making lists of unmanageable circumstances is not fun. I want to offer you a word of encouragement based on personal experience: God is doing a work in and with and through us, and he has good things in store for us—if we surrender to the process. God is totally non-codependent. God won't rush to our rescue as long as we want to stay our course of willful self-control. This doesn't mean God doesn't love and care about us, but God is not a "helicopter" parent—circling over us constantly giving us feedback so that we won't embarrass him or make mistakes. When we ask God for wisdom, scripture reports that God will move His mighty forces in the seen and unseen world to bless us (James 1). Can you think of at least one thing at this moment that you are grateful for and write a paragraph about your gratitude?

Prayer

Spoken words of sincere prayer are vital links to God. Sometimes I get tongue-tied, and could use a little help. Here's a recommended prayer:

Dear God, I, _____, admit that I am powerless and my life has become unmanageable. I ask for your help in my recovery. Denial has kept me from seeing how powerless I am and how unmanageable my life has become. I admit that I have at times lost hope. I've felt like I had few options and sometimes no good options. My view has been clouded by my despair, my shame, and my own efforts at self control. I choose to let go. I admit that I need your awesome power. Thank you, Father, for hearing my cry for help. Help me to begin to recognize your response. Amen.

Step 2

*We came to believe that
a power greater than ourselves
could restore us to sanity.*

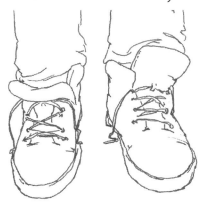

Introduction

Step two can be a stumbling block if we expect too much of ourselves. This step isn't asking us to have faith all figured out before we proceed. Instead, it is gently calling out to us a message that is both comforting and challenging. When I'm sitting around trying to figure out why I cannot sleep and am tempted to go back to my old eating disordered ways as a familiar, distracting, self-medication for my anxiety, my recovery has taught me how to pause to prepare. The skills I've learned by working these steps help me discover that what I'm really freaking out about is beyond my control. As a mother of three adults, I still find myself fretting over them as if I were in charge of their choices! As a daughter, I find myself now worrying about my parents' safety and well-being, much like I agonized when each of my children got their driver's licenses and hit the road solo for the first time. I am told I am currently in the exclusive club of the sandwich generation. If this means that I am supposed to feel squeezed by the cares and concerns of both the generation in front of me and the one running up behind me, then I guess that's an apt description.

The second step provides an immediate balm to my suffering. It teaches me that I am not alone. It teaches me that I have neither the power nor the responsibility for the care and proper management of others. And even in those situations where I find myself participating in problem solving, there is a power greater than those of us struggling to seek solutions, and this power is beneficent and restorative. In a nutshell, at this moment in the process, that's all this step is asking us to consider. Notice the verb tense—it's saying we "came to believe," meaning we don't have to have this higher power stuff all figured out. It is simply asking us to realize that there is a God, and we didn't get the job. We are not God. For me, that was part of my most profound work in step 2. I had to tell the truth—I am not God. I am not able or willing to know all, do all, or figure all of life out for myself and for others.

This step doesn't require us to have a lot of faith—just the willingness to be made willing. We were created to be and do much more than live a life of quiet desperation. As we move through this step, know that we are not alone. Others are praying for us. God tells us that He will redeem our life from the pit. From a former pit dweller, let me assure you—when God says He will do it, it will be done! Now go. Hurry. Watch and wait for God. Expect Him. He wants us to find Him!

Key Terms

Came to believe: "Coming to believe" is a process. We move from giving lip service to God's existence to a belief that I call "knowing that you know that you know." We were not created to live in a vacuum of unbelief. We were created to believe. It is part of the "eternity in our hearts" described by the author of Ecclesiastes:

I have seen the burden God has laid on men…He has also set eternity in the hearts of men; yet they cannot fathom what God has done from beginning to end. Ecclesiastes 3:10-11.

As the writer of Ecclesiastes points out, this belief is a messy, complex thing. That's why coming to believe is a process! Unless we grapple with the existence of the unseen world, it is my firmly held conviction that we cannot live well in the seen world. Most of us have been cheated out of our belief and the abundant life that accompanies radical believing. It is like our capacity to believe has been stolen. Jesus put it this way: "The thief comes only to steal and kill and destroy; I have come that they may have life, and have it to the full" (John 10:10). Our pasts have left many of us hurt and damaged. We're in bondage to a lot of lies—misuse of religion, cultic experiences, traditions that run counter to God's truth—and these harmful exposures leave us scarred. Now is the time to do three things:

1. Figure out what we truly believe.
2. See if our belief is false or true.
3. Decide to believe that which is true.

This is not an easy process. It invites us to become more conscious of how our beliefs and our behaviors do (or do not) "match up."

Power: In *Power To Choose*, Mike O'Neill says, "There's no power in something that you're supposed to believe but don't." To the extent that we believe, God is free to manifest divine power. God is thoroughly non-codependent. God doesn't bully us into belief. But when we believe, God's power is at work. I believe that God can transform me into my true God-created identity. But this doesn't mean I understand the implications of this belief. All I can honestly confess to on many days is that I believe in a God who has the power to transform, even if I find my faith confusing, disturbing, and even disruptive to my daily life. But when I think about this belief—the hope that God might choose to do for me what I cannot do for myself, freeing me from compulsions—that is pretty awesome.

Greater than ourselves: The truth is this: living on our own and acting independently of God, we're not doing so great…. are we? Jesus tells a hard truth. (Just because it's hard doesn't mean it isn't true!) He says this: "Apart from me you can do nothing" (John 15:5). We must break through the wall of denial and accept this truth: we haven't got the power, but if we will only believe, we can have access to it!

Sanity: In recovery communities, sanity is defined by implication. If we need restoration to sanity, the implication is that we are insane. One of my friends in recovery says that coming to understand that he was insane happened only by the grace of God. I agree. The tricky thing about insanity is that we rarely recognize it in ourselves. Here's a popular definition I've heard repeated so many times that I don't even know its origin: insanity is "doing the same thing over and over again expecting a different result." Sometimes it helps to remember what we said we were powerless over. Can we recognize how we keep attacking these issues and achieving the same frustrating results? Suppose we have an addiction issue. We're willing to make a lot of plans to control our using, but the plans never succeed. We still find ourselves powerless over our substance of choice. But we keep making plans, thinking that this time it will be different. That's insanity. Perhaps we know someone with an addiction issue. We've gone to great lengths to help them control their using. Unfortunately, the results are always the same. They use in spite of our best efforts. But we keep trying to control them. That's insanity.

Restore: Of all the key words in the twelve steps, this is my personal favorite. Restoration is an awesome, hopeful word. A few years ago, our community was hit hard by Tropical Storm Gaston. Our backyard looked like a bomb had exploded and we were at ground zero. Today, as I sit here writing, my window overlooks that same backyard. I can see my azaleas in full bloom; my knockout roses are knocking themselves out displaying their passionate pink glory; the grass is green and lush; the trees that didn't crash down upon us during the hurricane are thriving and spreading their branches over us in a protective, green canopy. My backyard has been restored. What once looked like a hopeless cause has been brought from death to life. It took a while, but it happened. This same restoration process can be true for you. That's the truth! In the Big Book (a book used frequently in Alcoholics Anonymous as a guide to sobriety), the benefits of step 2 are described in this way: "As we felt new power flow in, as we enjoyed peace of mind, as we discovered we could face life successfully, as we became conscious of His presence, we began to lose our fear of today, tomorrow, or the hereafter. We were reborn."

Do you long to be reborn? It can happen. But in order to experience this grand new way of living, we have to start by doing something different. Step 2 teaches us how. First, we come to believe...

Could: Sometimes the most important words sneak up on us. This step says that God could restore us. It does not say that God is obligated to do so. There are some conditions that must be met so that the restoration process can begin. These prerequisites are:

If we believe that there is a Higher Power, then act on what we believe.

End the distraction of unbelief. Simply begin believing what we say we believe, and ask God to continue to reveal more truth for us to live by. Sometimes people like to get theoretical about who God is and isn't. Put down obsessive thinking and simply start living what you believe.

God is not an abstract concept. God is not asking us to get excited about the idea of his existence. God is asking us to begin relating to him. God is real. God exists. God wants us to know him.

Neil Anderson says it like this: "Faith is the biblical response to the truth, and believing truth is a choice. Faith is something you decide to do, not something you feel like doing. Believing the truth doesn't make it true; it's true, so we believe it. Faith must have an object. It's not the idea that you merely "believe" that counts; it's what or whom you believe in that counts. Everyone believes in something, and everyone walks by faith according to what he or she believes. But if what you believe isn't true, then how you live won't be right." [5]

Step 2: Making It Personal

1) Read Isaiah 53 to learn about Jesus and Isaiah 46:9-11 to hear about God's commitment to his plan. Read Jeremiah 29:11 to read specifically about God's plans for your life. Read Psalm 34:18-22, Isaiah 40:28-31 and Isaiah 61:1-4 to see God's intentions toward people who are hurting. Read Psalm 100. I'm going to ask you a question that may be more complicated than it sounds. Please do not provide the 'right' answer, but take some time, pause to prepare before you respond: what do you believe about God? (Is he for you or against you; loving or lusting after your possessions; beneficent or angry; kind or cruel?)

2) Does your belief coincide with what you've just read in scripture?

3) Sometimes we hear a lot about God from others and assume that what they say is true. Sometimes we look at God through the filter of our life experience and make assumptions about God that are not true. Once I believed that God was a harsh taskmaster and my job was to work as hard as I could to earn his approval (conditional approval, always in danger of being withdrawn at the slightest misstep on my part). Work—work—work—do—do—do—no rest for the weary! I believed God was telling me I must perform and perform perfectly to be truly loved. Boy was I wrong! Read Matthew 11:28-30 and John 6:29. I was wrong about the kind of relationship God desired from me. What are some false beliefs about God and his relationship with you that you've discovered so far in your spiritual journey through the 12 steps?

4) In light of what you've read about God's character, what kind of relationship do you think God wants to have with you?

5) Read:

      Ezekiel 36:35
      Philippians 2:13(b)
      2 Corinthians 3:5

Who is it that has the power and does the work of restoration?

6) Reread John 6:29

What is your part? What is your work assignment?

7) Perhaps at this point in the study, you are tempted to think all this sounds too good to be true—at least for you. Read:
       Psalm 34:18-22
       Matthew 17:20
       Mark 9:23-24
       2 Corinthians 1:9

If you will but believe, these hope-filled words can be true for you! What have you read in this scripture study thus far that you truly believe?

8) I did not grow up in a home that spoke of God and the unseen world. It was easy for me to believe that the world evolved from primordial soup.

Read:
> Colossians 1:16
> Ephesians 1:11
> James 1:18

Did you know this? For many years I did not. (The great thing about families is that we can change. In recent decades, my extended family has come to know about God and many of us have awakened to the reality of this unseen world. If this can happen in my family, it can also happen in yours! It's really helped us learn how to love each other in more healthy and life-enriching ways.) When I discovered that I was indeed the most important of all the things God made, it gave me a reason to pause and re-evaluate my life. When I learned that God doesn't show favoritism, I was struck by how different God was from my experiences with mere mortals. I also discovered that the people in my life—no matter how annoying—are also valued highly by God. This rearranges my whole sense of relationship. This new information caused me to wrestle with my tendency to love things and use people. I acknowledge that sometimes I have allowed other people to use me. Step 2 is an opportunity for us to say: there is stuff about life and how it works that I don't understand, and I need to evaluate my relationships with God, self, and others.

Read:
> Psalm 139:15-16
> Ephesians 1:4
> Isaiah 46:2-4

What in these texts resonates most with your own thoughts and feelings?

9) Read John 8:32. Remind yourself of your points of bondage and the places in your life where you desire freedom. Notice that Jesus told his disciples in this passage that there was a condition to freedom: obedience. He said to them and to us that we will find our freedom as we choose to act on what we believe. How would you describe your own examples of bondage?

Prayer

Here's a recommended prayer:

Dear Lord, I, _____ , have come to believe
that you can restore me to sanity.
I realize that I need restoration.
I am in the process of coming to believe
that only you can offer me the opportunity for rebirth and restoration.
God, I do believe,
but like that father in the story Jesus told,
I also cry out this truth: "Help me in my unbelief."
I acknowledge that there is a lot I do not know about you
and that some of what I think I do know about you is probably false.
I thank you for the process and I am deeply grateful
that you are willing and able to give me a reborn life!
I pray for wisdom and for an open mind and heart,
so that I can come to a belief that is powerful
in its ability to renew my soul.
Amen.

Step 3

We made a decision to turn our life and will
over to the care of God as we understood him.

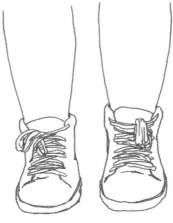

Introduction

"I know what I'm doing. I have it all planned out—plans to take
care of you, not abandon you, plans to give you the future you
hope for. When you call on me, when you come and pray to me,
I'll listen. When you come looking for me, you'll find me. Yes,
when you get serious about finding me and want it more than
anything else, I'll make sure you won't be disappointed."
(Jeremiah 29:11-14, *The Message*)

The third step requires that we make a decision to trust in a God who
promises all this and more:

> God knows what He's doing.
> God has a plan for your life.
> God promises never to abandon you.
> God promises to provide a future for you.
> God's future is hopeful. It is the abundant life.

These promises have a condition attached to them. This is our part. We
must call out to God. He promises to listen. I know that many of us may
have a history that teaches us that others do not listen when we call out.
But God listens whether others do or not.

I once believed that I would never find God. I thought he was for others but not for me. I was wrong. Here's the thing, though. I read this verse, and I did it, but I can't say that I had any expectations. The world had taught me that with few expectations come fewer disappointments. But I decided to try it. I simply sought God. I followed hard after God. I did it because I couldn't see any other options. I did it whether I was in the mood or not. I did it when it didn't make sense. I often did it poorly. Fortunately, this decision is not asking us to "get it right" or work harder. It's simply inviting us to face toward God and decide to give God a chance. Sound cheeky? Maybe, but I have experienced God as thoroughly secure, willing to embrace me, even in my cheekiness.

Please offer yourself the gift of patience. The loss of hope, the feelings of helplessness, the belief that nothing will ever change—none of these false beliefs formed in an instant. We get worn down like the hardest stone is eventually worn down with the slow and steady dripping of water. In this step we aren't trying to figure out our theology or our denominational loyalties. We aren't committing to church membership or strict adherence to a set of religious rules. We're just crying out. We're saying: "Hey, there is a God" (even though I am not sure what God is all about). We are saying: "I am not God, and I'm going to trust that Creator God knows more about how my life works than I have been able to figure out independently on my own power." That's it. It's simple, but not easy.

I was in a meeting room recently, and a young woman fresh out of her third rehab facility said the most profound thing. She said, "The twelve steps are a simple program for complicated people." The third step is choosing to simplify. It's firing ourselves from running our own lives and asking God to get down here and save us.

Key Terms

We made a decision: I don't know a verb tense that appropriately captures the on-going nature of this decision. Once I was baptizing a man who chose to reveal his decision publicly through baptism. This was a baptism by immersion—the way Jesus was baptized. First, he leaned back into the water. Once submerged, I helped lift him back out of the water, and up he arose! Pushing hair and water out of his face and shaking off the water like a shaggy dog, he peered at me and said, "Wow! I feel different. This was a good decision." I felt a little twinge of concern because the act of baptism is not magic. But a good decision is still a good decision.

Daily: On July 15, 1978, I married my husband. The entire ceremony lasted no longer than a good baptism. Each day, however, I recommit to the decision made during our marriage ceremony. The ceremony is not what keeps my husband and me married. We're married because we make a decision daily to be committed to each other. The initial decision is vital, but the relationship must also be continual. Prior to making a third-step decision, all of us experience the ebb and flow of emotional attachment to our past hurts, habits, and hang-ups. A decision frees us from the tyranny of these emotions. Consider this from Ephesians: "Then we will no longer be infants, tossed back and forth by the waves, and blown here and there by every wind of teaching and by the cunning and craftiness of men in their deceitful scheming" (Ephesians 4:14 NIV). This passage goes on to say that the outcome of a third-step decision is growth. James 1:6 puts it this way: "But when he asks, he must believe and not doubt; because he who doubts is like a wave of the sea, blown and tossed by the wind." Don't you want the tossing about to stop? Make a decision—accept God's help!

To turn our wills and our lives over: It is a beautiful sight to behold—the turning of a life and will over to the care of God. But there is often more process to it than most of us would care to admit. As my mother-in-law aged, her health required that she start turning things over. First, she had to give up her condo with the steep stairs. Eventually she moved into a wonderful community designed for people "of a certain age." It was a fight to the finish for her to acknowledge it was time to turn in her keys and stop driving. But her humility brought many of us greater peace and offered us the gift of a practical life lesson with faith implications. As I watched her humble herself to the aging process, what emerged was a woman of true dignity. She knew her body was made of dust but never was she more beautiful than in the last days of her life. Although she needed to trust others with her care, the by-product was a rich awareness of how much she was loved. I imagine it felt scary to her to trust like this, but this is the kind of attitude toward God to which faith calls us. It is as we turn things over that we discover how much God loves us.

To the care of God: What can I say to you about the care of God? God's very essence is love. God cares for us far more than we have ever cared for ourselves. When God looks at us, God doesn't just see our problems. God sees our potential. God knows what we are made of and why we were created. We were God's idea. We are the apple of God's eye—the best work God ever crafted. God is not only God-the-Creator (Bara in Hebrew) but also God-the-Healer (Rapha—Hebrew for healing, one stitch at a time). Life has dealt us some blows, and many of us have been taught some lies about who God is and what God's intentions are toward us. Allowing God to care for us and to teach us how to care for ourselves begins with the third step. I believe that over time, as we proceed down this path of growth and discovery, we will look back on our lives and exclaim: "God was here all along! Look how I was protected, guided, and saved! Yes, there are some who intended to harm me, but that was never God! God has taken the harm inflicted upon me and used it for good!"

As we understood Him: This phrase used to confuse me. I thought it meant that we could just make up a god that pleased us. That's not what this means. This phrase is expressing the very heart of the 12 steps: process. The only way we can relate to God is at the level at which we understand God. Through the process of working the 12 steps, our understanding will grow. But here's the really cool thing: God patiently accepts us wherever we are in the process just as God initially accepted Gideon. (See Judges 6 – 8 to read my favorite biblical illustration of this concept.) God accepted Gideon just where he was in his development, but didn't leave him stuck. God challenged, encouraged, and provided for Gideon to move from where he was to where God intended for him to be: Gideon the mighty warrior. I won't spoil the story for you, but I encourage you to go read it for yourself. It's awesome. Your job is to follow Gideon's lead and build a relationship of trust with God. God is not a theory or idea or concept or notion. God is real. And God wants a personal relationship with us.

My husband is slightly colorblind. Sometimes he wants to believe that a particular favorite shirt is navy blue. It is not. It is black. No amount of his understanding it to be blue will make it blue. The shirt is black. After lots of years of failing to trust my color sense over his own defective color vision, time has taught him to trust me. If he shows up for breakfast in a mismatched outfit, he is willing to go up and try again if I mention the color snafu. If you feel, as I once did, that you will never understand this

God stuff or if you have trouble believing that your vision of who God is might be impaired, fear not. God gives his wisdom freely to us, without finding fault. (See James 1.) Trusting can grow over time.

We have a mechanic that we trust. If he says our car needs major repairs, we thank him for finding the problem. We don't get a second or third opinion, waffle about what to do, or curse our misfortune at his hands. Why? Because we trust him. How did we come to trust him? It's because of our experience, through which we built a relationship. He never lets us down. When we decide to entrust our lives to the care of God, we are beginning a relationship that requires time and experience to build trust. Take the Gideon challenge. God will not disappoint. The mighty, miraculous, powerful working of God is not limited by our failure to understand. God is a loving God, whether we believe that or not. Be patient and persistent, and you'll be amazed at where God leads you!

Step 3: Making It Personal

Prepare yourself to be prepared. There are not a lot of questions in this section and there is a lot of scripture to read. Frankly, this is a simple step; you either "make a decision" or you do not. But it is a step fraught with danger. You may have believed lies about God, mistaking past hurtful life experiences as signs of an uncaring, unknowing, inactive God. Many of us have been taught false things about God. People sometimes do that in an effort to control us by causing us to live in fear.

What I think would be most helpful in this particular study is to take the recommended scripture readings and meditate on them. Write them on index cards. Ask God to show you the truths found in them. Ask: "If this is true, then what lies have I believed?" Wait for the answer. Expect to receive one from the God who gives so generously to all of us without finding fault. Ask God to prepare your heart to release lies that have kept you from turning your will and your life over to God's care. Make no mistake: this is a battle. Satan fights hard against us. He doesn't want us to be free. He doesn't want us to experience the abundant life that Christ so joyfully provides. (See John 10:10.) My prayer is that all who read and study this guide will be protected from the evil one so that they might find their way back to God.

1) Do you have a list of reasons why you have to take care of yourself and trust no one, including God? I want you to challenge that list by reading the following scriptures:

> Genesis 1:1, 31
> Exodus 14:14
> Psalm 139:15-16
> Jeremiah 29:11-14
> Isaiah 46:3-4
> Zephaniah 3:17
> Matthew 11:28-30
> John 3:16-17
> Ephesians 1:5

After reading these texts, can you list some examples that might help you accept that God is trustworthy?

2) Many people and things we have trusted have let us down. The result is disappointment, resentments and broken dreams. We can get stuck on the "wrongness" of what has happened in the past, or we can face facts: we have put our trust in people, places, or things that were never intended to carry the weight of our expectations. Read:

Psalm 118:8
Romans 6:12-14
Romans 8:1-3
Galatians 2:17-21
Ephesians 1:11
Philippians 3:7-9

Have you become more trusting of God? Can you genuinely make this decision to turn everything over to him? If you cannot say you are ready for a full commitment, are there some things that you can turn over to God (list them)?

3) Read:

> Psalm 143:10-11
> Proverbs 3:5-6
> Matthew 6:24
> John 6:29
> Romans 10:9-13
> 2 Corinthians 6:2

Are you ready to commit? Anyone can say they're willing. Test yourself on this. Think about turning over your relationships, problems, finances, children, parents, angers, fears, resentments, lust, greed, etc. Are there any items on this list that you are *not* yet willing to turn over? If so, make a list of these items.

4) Spend some time thinking about what you will get out of this new relationship with God. Read:

> 2 Chronicles 16:9
> Proverbs 16:3
> Isaiah 61:10
> John 3:36

Think about your life as a small business. Prior to this step, you've been Chief Executive Officer, Chief Financial Officer, Head of Human Resources, Director of Marketing and Sales, Secretary, Receptionist, and Custodian. You've been your number one client, and your number one competition. You've done it all. According to business reports written by independent, objective observers, your business is in the tank. You're sinking fast. You are freaked out, insecure, neurotic, and emotional. You want to give up, but you can't see a way out. You're at the end of your rope. Along comes the owner of the best business in your field. He offers to take you into his company. It's a family-owned business, and he wants to adopt you into his family. You'll have to set aside all those fancy titles and simply be willing to be the owner's child. But you've got to decide: Am I willing to give up my way and be adopted into this new family? You do your research, and you discover that this offer is unbelievable—this is the best parent ever. He treats all his children as if they are his favorite, because they truly are. There is absolutely no telling what will come from this relationship, but according to irrefutable sources, he knows each of his children better than they know themselves. Once you are his, He will equip and train, guide and direct. All his kids live out an awesome adventuresome life for which they were custom designed.

What did you hear from the scripture readings, and how might that influence your decision?

Prayer

Spoken words of sincere prayer are vital links to God. Sometimes I get tongue-tied and could use a little help. Here's a recommended prayer. It is my prayer that you can pray this with meaning. Remember, you were created to believe! This prayer works best when spoken aloud, in the presence of another person. I have found that for most of us, we end up on our knees when we begin our intimate, prayerful relationship with God. I wish I could be with you when you pray this prayer. Whomever you invite to join you in this decision-speaking process will count it among the grandest privileges they will ever be granted. Know that our spirits join and heaven sings as you pray.

Lord, I humbly surrender my life to you.
I confess that my life is unmanageable,
and that on my own, independently of you,
I have found myself in trouble.
I don't even understand how all this happened.
I don't think I even grasp the full meaning of a surrendered life.
There's a man in the Bible who cried out,
"Lord, I believe; help me in my unbelief."
God, I can relate to that man!
 I thank you that you are so gracious and merciful
that none of this is held against me.
Take my life, Lord, lead me,
so that I might experience times of refreshment.
May all of my life be lived in accordance
with your will and your purpose for me.
I now turn my will and my life over to your care.

Amen

Step 4

We made a searching and fearless
moral inventory of ourselves.

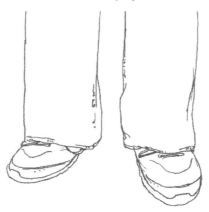

Introduction

If you have made it this far in the 12-step journey, you have made peace with God. That's an important step. It enables us to recognize that shame-based living isn't the way Prince and Princess Warriors (a.k.a. Kids of the King) live. Hopefully, we're learning, we're coming to believe, we're in the process of accepting the very character and sovereignty of God. We're allowing these truths to embolden us, to encourage us, and to humble us.

The fourth step requires courage. It prepares us for the next stage of the process: making peace with ourselves. Thankfully, God did not give us a spirit of timidity but of power, love, and sound mind. We're going to need God's power, God's love, and the mind of Christ to take this next step.

I find that self-objectivity is a difficult task. It feels burdensome at times. But learning how to see myself accurately enables me to understand how others see me. Why is this so crucial for our God-created identity? From the beginning of time, God had us in mind and created us as relational beings. We weren't meant to live in isolation. In Genesis we read that the first thing God said was "not good" in his created kingdom was that man was alone.

In the New Testament, a crowd of people asked Jesus what is the most important commandment. He gave them two answers: love God, and love others as you love yourself. Isn't that fascinating? He didn't command them to achieve world peace, end poverty, or fight for the rights of the underprivileged. That's not what he said. He said "love." Loving God, self, and others is all about relationships. I believe that world peace, the cessation of poverty, and fighting for the rights of the underprivileged are all awesome passions to pursue. We know, though, that they stem from love. Jesus knew that if we would love God, self, and others we would be ready, willing, and able to fight for any cause God set before us.

We can't live out the two most important commandments if we are incapable of living in relationship with others. First, we can't love others if we have not made peace with ourselves. Second, we will struggle to live lovingly with others if we do not understand how others perceive us.

Today I was walking out of a store, and my son evidently watched me trudge across the parking lot. When I climbed in the car, he asked:

"Mom, are you okay?"

"Yes, I'm fine. Why do you ask?"

"Your face looked kind of stressed."

"It did? Thanks for telling me. I was just thinking. My face wasn't matching my insides because my insides are really happy."

He continued, "You know, my friends say that I'm going to have a permanent wrinkle across my face because they say I walk around looking stressed." He said this with that tone we use when we're in the middle of an insight.

"Huh," I said. "I guess that's why I often ask you if you're stressed when I pick you up from school. I wonder if you and I share that trait. When we're thinking, I wonder if other people see us and think we're stressed out."

"I asked my friends, 'What do you want me to do, look like this?'" He made an exaggerated happy face that could not possibly be considered an upgrade in facial expressions. I laughed. He's a funny guy.

"I don't know what the solution is, but you and I have both learned something about ourselves today. If our facial expressions don't match how we feel in our hearts, we will confuse other people. I guess we both need to work on making our outsides and insides match."

"I guess." He was finished with this conversation.

I realize what a valuable lesson I learned today, thanks to my son. These kinds of lessons and more await us as we enter into the fourth-step process. Sometimes you may be reluctant to continue the journey, but I want to encourage you to press on.

I often think of the Old Testament character, Gideon, when I think about the fourth step. Gideon was a guy willing to do a fourth step. Prior to his remarkable encounter with his true God-created self, he was hiding out in a cave. He believed himself to be the runt of his litter—the least in his clan—born to a clan that was the least of all clans. But God saw him differently:

"...The Lord is with you, mighty warrior."
(Judges 6:12 NIV)

Gideon didn't believe this message from the Lord, but he went on to do a partial fourth step. He named his shortcomings, and I suppose he expected the angel to agree. I wonder if he just thought the angel would say, "Yeah, you're right, dude. Sorry to bug you." Did he then expect the angel just to leave him there, hiding in his cave of desperation?

Read Judges 6 and see what happens to Gideon. It is awesome. He becomes the mighty warrior he was created to be. It wasn't easy, but God gently guided him through his defects and revealed to Gideon his potential.

One of my friends who is helping write these study guides wants me to mention another important truth. He says that it is important to remember that God will gently guide us through this uneasy process. God will also provide us with the strength and honesty that we do not believe we have in us or are capable of ever having. I like that. Another reminder is that it is God who makes us both willing and able to do his good work!

Key Terms

How to make an inventory: Three descriptions of the process that I have found helpful are 1) The description of the fourth step in *Power to Choose*, by Mike O'Neill. You can find this resource listed in the back of this study guide. Mike offers a wonderful and comprehensive guide for completing a fourth step. I recommend it for further clarity on the fourth step process. 2) The description on pages 64-71 of *The Big Book of Alcoholics Anonymous*: this is the original approach suggested for a fourth step. 3) On pages 68-74 of Melody Beattie's book, *Codependents' Guide to the Twelve Steps*, you will find her description of the process. There are other ways to do an inventory. The most important part of this process is that we actually do it. Almost everyone emphasizes the importance that an inventory be done in writing and without us stopping to evaluate our writing in the middle of the process. It is kind of like a written "life review," so don't hesitate to include remembrances from childhood. Here are some approaches that I have found to be helpful:

Write a list of all the people, institutions, or principles that you resent, and why. Explain how you feel these people, institutions or principles have harmed you.

Write a list of all your fears. Write down why you fear people, institutions, or principles and explain how your fears have harmed you.

Make a list of all your grudges and injuries (real or imagined). Include in this list all the harm others have done to you. Some people hesitate, thinking that theirs are grudges or injuries unworthy of being mentioned. Don't filter your inventory—just write! Complain and whine all you want. The rest of the process will put an end to this self pity, so don't hold back now!

Make a list of all the problem areas in your life. Common areas of concern are: finances, sex, marriage, work, etc.

Write a list of all the things you've done that have resulted in your feeling guilty. Include all the people, institutions, etc. that you have harmed. Again, don't pre-filter your list. Sometimes we have false guilt—that's guilt that really belongs to someone else. God's word teaches us that "there is no condemnation for those who are in Christ Jesus." (Romans 8:1). This step will help clarify these confusing issues.

List your assets. It's like doing inventory at a store. See what's there and write it down. One of the positive things that I recorded on my first inventory was how I changed my relationship with food once I knew it was unhealthy. I also considered it an asset that I was always seeking a better way to live. You have assets too. so write them down. (Sometimes it's harder to include the assets.)

Another recommended list is very simple: write down anything that upsets you, bothers you, bugs you, or gets under your skin. It's good to report how this makes you feel and what you believe about bothersome situations.

As you make all these lists, it is important to do so with a spirit of self-acceptance rather than shame. Your list of wrongdoings will probably increase your awareness that you have harmed others. That will not feel good. But treating yourself badly is not the solution. The attitude of self-condemnation helps no one. It hinders the recovery process just as profoundly as failing to admit legitimate wrongdoing.

Searching: It's important to write down what you really feel and do. I know that it's tempting to write down what you think you *should* feel and do. But presenting a false self is cheating. This search is not just an exercise in navel gazing. It is one step in a process designed to equip you to be your true, God-created self. An old bumper sticker claims that "God don't make no junk." That's true, but if we're living like junkyard dogs, then how can our true God-created identity shine through? As you search, know that your "pile of junk" can never exceed God's amazing grace, mercy, and love. Fuel your search with the knowledge that good things come when we get real with God.

One word of caution: as you are working through this step, keep it personal and private. Step 5 will provide an opportunity to share and interact with others about what you're writing down. As you search, just write. Don't try to figure out what you're writing. Don't judge yourself or make excuses. Most of us develop reactionary patterns of behaving simply as coping strategies. No one wakes up every morning and says, "How can I mess up my life today?" Just write. Remember, all you're doing is making the inventory. Now is not the time to think ahead; just make the list. I would suggest that you write as if no one will ever look at this list.

Fearless: Someone famous said that courage is not the absence of fear, but the willingness to act in spite of it. I like to remember the verse "God did not give us a spirit of timidity, but a spirit of power, of love and of self-discipline" (2 Timothy 1:7 NIV). When Paul wrote this verse to his apprentice, Timothy, he was specifically trying to encourage Timothy to use his spiritual gifts and open up and show his God-created identity to the world. Perhaps you're wondering what there is to fear if all we're talking about is showing off the good stuff. Maybe you're thinking that it's such a hassle to inventory all this old junk. Why not start fresh and just forget about all that past pain? The reason is simple: it doesn't work. As you search, consider this: your "small living"— your patterns of "less than" behaving—are masks for the real you. Ultimately, I am encouraging you, as Paul encouraged Timothy, to allow God to strip away the patterns that you have chosen for your life and to allow God to restore your life to the abundant, prosperous, peaceful, rested life God desires for you. Allow God to pick your patterns for large living.

Moral inventory: "A moral inventory is a list of our weaknesses and our strengths. This inventory is something we prayerfully accomplish with God's help. It is for our benefit."[6] It is important to remember that this is a moral inventory, not just a behavioral inventory! These lists are not focused on what we are *doing* as much as they are designed to show us who we are *being*. My pattern of eating in weird ways was just a symptom of underlying defects. When I took my inventory, I discovered a lot of anxiety kept popping up in my writing. The weird eating got my attention, but simply changing my eating wasn't going to solve my life problems. Until I was willing to deal with the real problem, I wasn't going to find a lasting solution. What does that mean? It means that I may change my weird eating but I will replace it with some other equally ineffective strategy for managing my anxiety.

God doesn't want our emotions *managed*; he wants them resolved. O'Neill says: "Emotions are like visitors: they're supposed to show up, tell you something, and then they're supposed to leave." [7] If we don't resolve our emotions, then they don't leave. They hang around and become the roots of all kinds of unhealthy behaviors that ultimately require us to do more fourth step work. Since I have turned my life and will over to the care of God, I know that when I feel anxiety it is a signal. The anxiety alerts me to take an inventory. It reveals to me that I am not fully embracing steps 2 and 3. The inventory process provides me with information so that I am able to gain renewed insight and continue working through the steps.

As you begin step 4, consider these as possibilities for things to inventory: anger, lust, greed, jealousy, laziness, paranoia, depression, anxiety, insecurity, irresponsibility, lying, pride, oversensitivity, apathy, rationalization, self-pity, gossip, ingratitude, rudeness, rigidity, judgmental attitudes, complaining, evasiveness, dishonesty, control, over-compliance, violence, and more.

Of ourselves: Yesterday I had in a lengthy conversation with a person who had relapsed. There were a lot of reasons: life was too stressful, the boss fired him, no one would give him a ride to a meeting, nobody would lend him money to pay the rent and on and on. He was doing a pretty good job of making an inventory of other people's problems. But a fourth step is not an inventory of other people's stuff. A fourth step inventory is a personal evaluation of our own stuff. In Lamentations 3:40, we are told to examine our ways, test them, and return to the Lord. No mention is made of examining others. In 1 Corinthians 11:28, we're told to examine ourselves before we take communion. Self-examination is a spiritual practice. Self-examination is not the same as being self-focused. Living a self-focused life gets us into trouble! But self-examination helps us get clear about the kinds of changes that we need to make. Honestly, we all would like it if we could skip this step. Some of us avoid this step by pretending that we don't have anything to inventory. Some of us avoid it by being so overwhelmed with the feelings of shame and inadequacy that we just can't get started. Either response tends to make us run from the process, but step 4 is absolutely essential. It will help anyone who enters into the 12-step process break the cycle of shame-based living.

Step 4: Making It Personal

1) Read Psalm 139:15, 23-24. Also read 1 John 4:8-9. It is difficult to see ourselves accurately. What can we learn from these texts?

2) We don't complete a moral inventory so that we can earn God's love. We do it because we've made a decision to turn our lives and our wills over to God's care and control. This requires us to examine our lives in light of new information. The new information is that we are the apple of God's eye. God has big plans for us. So an inventory is like spring cleaning. It's getting us ready for the good stuff God wants to bring our way! You are in the process of transformation. Ask God to show you both your assets and liabilities. Ask Him to show you the person you were created to become.

Read:

       Ephesians 4:17-25
       Galatians 5:13-18
       Mark 7:20-23

What have you learned from these scriptures that will help you when you take your inventory?

3) Taking an inventory is not easy! Read:
     Job 33:33
     Lamentations 3:21-33
     Ezekiel 36:26-27 and 31
     Romans 12:1-3
     1 John 1:8-9

What hope is available to us? What would your life be like if you could know and do God's good, pleasing and perfect will?

4) Read:
     2 Corinthians 7:10
     1 John 3:18-22

What is the difference between worldly sorrow and godly sorrow? Can you think of a time when you've been sorry about something—but not willing to admit you were wrong? Write out some examples of both 'worldly sorrow' and 'godly sorrow.' Notice the differences between them. Notice also that God never condemns us. The Holy Spirit convicts, but never condemns. We've previously studied scriptures that tell us how we can have a faulty perspective. Your heart, when filled with shame and condemnation, gives you a faulty reading. Spend some time thinking about how a heart filled with shame and condemnation can actually hinder the recovery process.

Can you write a few lines about your own experiences with shame?

5. Read:

> Genesis 4:2-7
> Psalm 81:11-12
> Psalm 106:15
> Hosea 8:7
> Galatians 6:7
> Matthew 6:24
> 1 Corinthians 10:21

Gravity is a law of nature that we take for granted. The seasons come and go, and we take that for granted. Here's another law: the law of cause and effect. Nothing changes if nothing changes. Your actions cause a reaction. Can you write down an example of this principle in your own life?

6. Read:

> Proverbs 28:13
> Job 7:11
> 1 Corinthians 11:28
> James 1:5

Is there anything in these texts which might help you be ready to begin your inventory?

Prayer

Here's a recommended prayer:

Father God, may the words of my mouth
and the meditation of my heart be pleasing in your sight,
O Lord, my Rock and my Redeemer.
Lord, you've said that I can know the truth,
and that the truth will set me free.
I long for truth.
Free me from my false beliefs.
Allow me to see myself as you see me.
You've told me that there is a way that seems right to a man,
but in the end it leads to death.
I know this from personal experience.
My way has not resulted in abundant, peaceful, prosperous living.
Teach me your ways, so that I can tell the difference
between my misguided strategies and your solutions.
Show me the truth, Father, about myself.
Reveal to me my wrongs, but also my strengths.
Show me your complete picture of me—the good and the bad.
I have messed up my life, and I am incapable of fixing it.
I am committed to writing down my wrongs,
the wrongs others have done to me,
and also those things that I have done right.
I ask you to give me the strength and the courage to complete the task.
I am trusting that you will keep your promises to me,
making all things right.
Thank you Lord, for restoring me!
Amen.

Step 5

*We admitted to God, to ourselves,
and to another human being
the exact nature of our wrongs.*

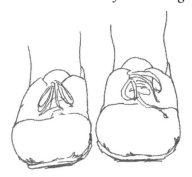

Introduction

One of my favorite stories is found in the first book of the Bible—Genesis 18. Three strangers came to visit Abraham. It seems as if two were angels, and one was the Lord himself. The Lord prophesies his return in one year and promises that Abraham's wife, Sarah, will birth a son by the time he returns. Sarah is doing what any good wife would do. She's eavesdropping. She hears the Lord's pronouncement, and she laughs! Sarah has been barren her entire life. She and Abraham "were already old and advanced in years," according to this account. Evidently Sarah thought bearing a child at her age was utterly preposterous. She was worn out. Her husband was old. Certainly it was too late to hope for the satisfaction of bearing a child. (If you've read the story you know that she does get pregnant.)

But that's not my favorite part. My favorite part is when she failed to admit her laughter. The Lord asked Abraham why Sarah laughed. She lied and said, "I did not laugh."

The Lord said, "Yes, you did laugh."

"I did not!"

"Did too!"

"Did not!"

"Did too!"

I chuckle every time I picture this exchange. I think this is the first "He said/she said" conversation recorded in history. I review this story every time I am about to work Step 5. Like Sarah, I have trouble "admitting" things to God, to myself, and to others. I'm not sure which is the toughest part—myself, God, or another human. I simply have trouble "admitting" things—even things that aren't all that bad.

Sarah laughed. That's all. Was that so bad? A critic might say it was an indication of her lack of faith in God. Maybe so. God had promised she would have a child. Why didn't she believe God's messenger? If you and your husband were way past the average childbearing years and someone told you that you were going to have a child, wouldn't you be tempted to laugh (or cry, depending on your view)? Did she know the stranger was actually the Lord? Perhaps she did. But hasn't God spoken promises to you that you haven't believed? Aren't there rich truths of hope and healing in God's word that you have ignored or that you believed applied only to others? I think we can extend Sarah some grace. I hope you will also be gentle with yourself during this process. Admitting to God, self, and others the exact nature of our wrongs is tough work. If you ask, God will eagerly give you the strength and willingness to do this step, but it's still a painful step. My prayer is that you will find the right person to listen to your inventory.

Key Terms

Admit: Most unhealthy family systems share a common goal: never let 'em see you sweat. That's another way of saying that "the best defense is a good offense." In families with hurts, habits, and hangups (that includes almost all families), admission is sometimes viewed as a weakness. Why is admitting the error of our ways so tough? Unhealthy family systems are usually not safe places to reveal a weakness. Unhealthy families tend to be chaotic, capricious, and inconsistent. They can be rigid and rule-driven or without guidance entirely. Love in such families is conditional and life is unpredictable. Discipline is sporadic and sometimes cruel.

Even in healthy families, children can learn (usually due to unintentional teaching) that being yourself is not a good idea. When I was a child, I loved to read. I was so excited about the wonderful world of books! I couldn't wait to share what I learned from my reading every night during dinner. I assumed everyone would be as thrilled as I was by my adventures through the written word. As an adult, I look back on that time and realize how boring that must have been for everyone else. In my enthusiasm, I recounted every plot twist and detail of that day's book. I thought I was sharing a priceless gem. My family did not share this view. They teased me about my reading. They rolled their eyes and laughed. Soon I stopped sharing. No one intended any harm. They just wanted a moment of peace. But, from my child's view, I concluded that I was not safe in this family of teasers. I think it served as confirmation of a vulnerability all humans experience, a fear that we are "less than." I developed a strongly held conviction that something was broken within me and being myself was not a good thing. So I ask you: was I a kid, teen, young adult, middle-aged mom, who was willing to admit a shortcoming? Certainly not! I learned, as many of us do, that to share the "real me" invites shaming—intentional or otherwise. If we learn that being ourselves is not okay, how much harder is it to admit when we have been our "bad" (or wrong, or mistaken, or simply less than the best) self? I cannot adequately convey the beauty of the cleansing experience I had when I shared with God, myself, and another for the first time. Admitting the exact nature of our wrongs is a hard thing to do. It is made tougher by past admissions gone wrong. But in the right environment—having come to know the awesome, loving God of scripture—it can be a comforting time of healing.

To God, to ourselves and to another human being: Listen to how the biblical text talks about confession:

Are you hurting? Pray. Do you feel great? Sing. Are you sick? Call the church leaders together to pray and anoint you with oil in the name of the Master. Believing-prayer will heal you, and Jesus will put you on your feet. And if you've sinned, you'll be forgiven—healed inside and out. Make this your common practice: Confess your sins to each other and pray for each other so that you can live together whole and healed. The prayer of a person living right with God is something powerful to be reckoned with. (James 5:13-16 *The Message*)

One day I confessed a pretty minor shortcoming in church. I told a silly story about how I was bad at remembering to attach a document when sending out an email. I told this in the context of a message I was teaching on grace. My point had to do with love covering a multitude of sins. I shared with the congregation how my entire team knew that I was a goof about this. I'd send out an email and tell them something was attached, and they'd send back a reply asking if it was written in invisible ink. My shortcoming, I reported, has to do with a lack of attention to detail. But my team loves me anyway. That was my point. But I think God had a different point. Since the day I confessed this shortcoming, I have remembered to attach documents I send out most of the time. Weird. Now sometimes I get emails back saying, "Hey, what's up with you? You attached your document!" Through this event, God reminded me that when we confess something and bring it into the light, powerful things happen. I desire to admit my shortcomings more than ever because I have been given a superficial but powerful-to-me example of the power of God to work through even the silliest of confessions. I don't know why or how this change in my ability to attach a document to an email occurred, but I know *who* made it possible. God is in the business of restoration. He is Rapha God—healing us, one stitch at a time (Rapha is Hebrew meaning healing, one stitch at a time).

Choosing someone to hear our confession needs to be done with care. Make sure it is someone with whom you can be frank, open, and honest. Ideally, it is best to share with someone who has worked through the 12-step process. If we don't know anyone with 12-step experience, look for someone who is willing to be available, who listens well, and who can relate to your struggles. I think it's important for the person to be the same gender. Sometimes this person may need to speak a word of encouragement and accountability, so it's best to find someone to whom we are willing to listen.

The exact nature of our wrongs: The most important aspect of the admission process is to eliminate secrecy. It's a challenge to admit the exact nature of our wrongs. That's why it is important and very beneficial to have an experienced listener. As we go down our fourth step inventory, our encourager will need to help us stay on track. New insights will be revealed and we will need to add them in writing to our original inventory. An excellent listener will be tuning in to hear the exact nature of our wrongs. After listening to our feelings of resentment, anxiety and fear, hearing our reactions and patterns of responding, and reading our lists, we will have a much-improved working knowledge of ourselves. Trust me, it will be a huge relief to have shared this with God, self, and another.

Mike O'Neill suggests in his book, *Power to Choose*, that we finish the fifth step and go off by ourselves and take time for quiet, prayerful reflection. He recommends reviewing the first five steps and then making time to be alone with God. As we read and review, listen for God's voice. We may need to add something to our list, go back to our trusted listener, and tell that person what we forgot. Once we can honestly say that the process is as complete as possible at this time, the fifth step is finished!

As an example of how telling the truth about the exact nature of our wrongs can make a difference, consider this statement from an interview with Corrie ten Boom. She spent many years in a Nazi concentration camp. She was a Christian, imprisoned for being a sympathizer to the Jewish people. This is what she says about telling the truth:

The special temptation of concentration-camp life—the temptation to think only of oneself, took a thousand cunning forms. I knew this was self-centered, and even if it wasn't right, it wasn't so very wrong, was it? Not wrong like sadism and murder and the other monstrous evils we saw every day. Was it coincidence that joy and power drained from my ministry? My prayers took on a mechanical ring. Bible study reading was dull and lifeless, so I struggled on with worship and teaching that had ceased to be real. Until one afternoon when the truth blazed like sunlight in the shadows. And so I told the group of women around me the truth about myself—my self-centeredness, my stinginess, my lack of love. That night real joy returned to my worship. [8]

Step 5: Making It Personal

1) Read:

     Psalm 32:1-5
     Proverbs 28:13
     1 John 1:8-10

Make a list of everything you can learn from these texts about the benefits of a fifth step. What does the psalmist say his life was like before he took his fifth step? How do these truths relate to your current situation?

2) Read Luke 12:2-3.

Secrets must be given up to work a fifth step effectively. Recently I was called to a home where a family was in crisis. The drug addicted family member was in bad shape. There were some legal issues involved too. It was decided that placement in a treatment facility was the best option. As we drove toward the facility, the antsy dependent person was worried about one thing: what if somebody found out they were in treatment? Denial is a powerful hindrance to freedom. This person weighed about 90 pounds, had tics and severe agitation, had been caught breaking into homes and robbing family members, neighbors, and friends. There was a public arrest and the drug possession charge (among others) was reported in the local paper. I asked my new friend: "Who doesn't know you need treatment? You?" Sometimes we kid ourselves that others don't know our secrets. My experience says bad news travels fast. What secrets have you feared would be exposed?

3) Read:

> Proverbs 20:9
> James 5:13-16
> Galatians 6:1-4
> Hebrews 4:12-16
> Romans 3:23

Sometimes we come to believe that we are alone in our wrongdoing, or we resist acknowledging that we've done wrong. What do these scriptures tell us? What are the implications? (Hint: We're not alone. Whom do you know who has been in your situation? How can you enlist that person's support and wise counsel? Make a list of possibilities.)

4) Read 2 Timothy 3:1-5

The writer tells us that bad behavior is going to happen. Notice the last phrase, "having a form of godliness…" So even spiritual people are vulnerable to bad behavior! Why? Every pattern has a perceived payoff. In step 4 you identified some cycles of responding to life situations. Ask God to show you what your payoff has been. What benefits have you gotten from your fears, resentments, and offenses?

5) Read John 3:19-21
What do you want to keep in the dark? What light are you hoping to avoid?

6) Read:
    1 Peter 2:11-12
    Galatians 5:1
    Jeremiah 29:12-14

What payoffs does God promise us when we choose to live as his children? How do God's promised payoffs compare to your perceived payoffs? Pray about this. Take a good, hard look at your life choices. How are your choices working for you?

Prayer

I know that I am often guilty of sloppy praying. In my prayer time each day, I have a set time for confession—agreeing with God about my sins. Sin at its core is living independently of God. My bad behaviors are a symptom of my independent living, but I can also fool myself into believing I am without sin. Even "good" behaving is sin when it is done independently of God. For example, teaching a Bible study is a good thing to do, right? But if I'm doing it to win the approval of others, then that is sin. (See James 4:1-10.) I must confess that sometimes I am careless and rushed, and I pray: "Lord, You know everything about me—even the number of hairs on my head. I know that you know what I've done wrong, and how I've lived independently of you. Please forgive me for all my sins, even the ones I don't know I've committed." A quick prayer is better than no prayer, I suppose, but it is also a sloppy prayer.

How would my husband respond if he came home from work, and I told him I had a confession to make? He would sit down slowly and wait. He would speculate and wonder, "What did she do now?" Then, suppose I said, "Honey, I've done something wrong today; would you forgive me?" Would he say, "Sure, no problem"? I don't think so! He wouldn't know whether I ran over the cat, had an affair, or bought two expensive coffees in one day! He would probably say: "What did you do?" How would my husband like it if I responded: "Well, it was really, really bad. Trust me. But I'm in kind of a hurry to get dinner on the table, so would you just forgive me?" If it wouldn't work with my spouse, why do we think it will work with God? Effective, intimate relationships require intentional conversations. The problem with sloppy praying is not that God needs the specifics, but we do. We need to take the time and have the discipline to think long and hard about our daily living.

It will be important to be alert and on guard. Have you ever gone on a weight loss program that required you to "weigh in" in front of someone? Experts tell us that a high level of accountability, such as "weighing in," speeds weight loss. Which would be more effective: "weighing in" or reporting in? Obviously, the scales don't lie. They are very specific. It's the same with prayer. Step 5 teaches us to pray specifically. Here's a recommended prayer to get you started. After this prayer, I suggest you begin talking to God using your own words. Go over your fourth step with great detail. Talk aloud. Speak the words of that fourth step. After you and God have the big discussion, you will be better prepared to share this same inventory with another person.

Dear Lord, I am ready to be real with you.
I know that this is part of the process
that is going to free me from all my bondage.
Teach me to tell you the truth.
Amen.

Step 6

*We were entirely ready to have God
remove all these defects of character.*

Introduction

What do you think it means to be "entirely ready" to have God remove our defects of character? If we know our defects, and want them gone, what does it take to be "entirely ready"? A timid knock on my office door introduced me to a young woman who knows what it means to be "entirely ready." It's been two years since she made her escape from a family system riddled with substance abuse, physical abuse, and neglect. In the beginning, it was hard. She missed her family, even though she knew something was wrong at home. She left to save herself, but sometimes she wondered why.

Then she met the man of her dreams—or so she thought. Instantly she felt a cosmic connection and she just *knew* that he was the one for her. Such assurance and confidence in her newfound love emboldened her, and she joyfully accepted his suggestion to move in together at her place. It made such perfect sense. They'd save more money and would get around to getting married someday soon. No rush, really—after all, he was her destiny.

Until she got pregnant and he split. Sometimes he came around, and she was thrilled. She decided that the pregnancy was indeed a shock to him, and he just needed time to sort things out. The only certainties for her were these: he was her destiny, and he would return soon. Friends told her he had acquired a new love, but she decided they were just jealous of this special bond that she shared with the love of her life. She told them: "If you only knew how he treats me when we're alone, you'd know how much he loves me!"

She continued to be "entirely ready" to accept his lame excuses and erratic behavior. Months passed. She waited patiently for the return of her destiny. When the baby arrived, he showed up and got a big kick out of pointing out his newborn son to family and friends. She smiled with delight. She thought to herself, "I was right! I knew he'd return."

Unfortunately, he forgot to pick them up from the hospital and she felt totally humiliated. She called a friend to come take her home. She thought that there was no limit to her shame until she walked in the apartment and found her knight with another damsel. When the dust cleared and all the company fled, she confronted him. She'd never done this before and was shocked when he smacked her hard across the face, almost causing her to drop her newborn infant.

She now tells me that it was at that moment when she realized that she may have left the abusive home in which she grew up only to recreate it with this man. She wants to know what suggestions I have for her. She doesn't want to end up like her mother. She says that she is open to any ideas I might offer her except one: she cannot live without this man. She is "entirely ready" to do anything it takes to help him understand that she is the one for him. She would also like for him to stop reminding her so much of her own father.

She shook her head in confusion and said that she just doesn't get it. She doesn't know how to be "entirely ready." I assure her that being "entirely ready" is one of the things she does best. I pointed out her readiness to accept this man as her savior. In so doing, she willingly submitted herself to him. At this point in time, this young woman has spent one entire year being "entirely ready" to live any way this man dictated.

So here's a hard question: who or what are you "entirely ready" for? Notice that this step does not say "entirely ready" to go to any lengths to remove my defects of character. Some of us have been ready and willing to be done with our defects of character for a long time. That's not what this step says. It says: "entirely ready to have God..."

Are we "entirely ready" to let God be in charge of our lives? Are we "entirely ready" to let God do for us what we have never been able to do for ourselves? Are we "entirely ready" to have God transform our lives from the inside out?

It really would be a sight to behold if all of us were as ready to have God as this young lady was to have the man of her dreams.

Key Terms

Entirely ready: God does an awful lot for us in the sixth step. But we must be willing to let him. This step is a paradox. It is passive, in that we are preparing to ask God to remove our defects of character. But it is also active and powerful, because willingness compels us to act. When our daughter was three years old, she loved the idea of jumping into the pool. She loved to practice. "Look mommy, I'm jumping into the pool!" she squealed, as she jumped off our couch onto the cushy, carpeted floor. If we weren't at the pool, she was begging to go. But once we got there she was skittish about jumping in. She wanted to jump, but she just wasn't quite ready. Eventually the blue water enticed her, and she became willing to jump. Oh, the joy! Oh, the delight on her face the day she made her first jump! She's all grown up now, and she's a terrific swimmer. But none of her accomplishments have ever seemed as profound as the first time she became willing to be made willing. You can know this joy too—when you are entirely ready. We are entirely ready when we get to the point that we're willing to jump into God's arms and ask him to take us on a new journey—a grand, epic adventure where we allow God to remove our defects of character.

God remove: Apart from God, we can do nothing. You can be as sincere, as passionate, as purposeful as anyone has ever been. But on our own and independent of God, we are incapable of self-transformation. Only God transforms. Only God saves. Only God frees us from the bondage of trying to save ourselves. Only God can accomplish the complete rebuilding of self. What this step is asking of us is this: believe that without God's help, we can do nothing. Then, prepare to accept his help.

All defects of character: Whatever we choose to call them, character defects are those undesirable parts of ourselves that must be removed if we are going to be our real, God-created selves. They are our faults, shortcomings, failings, manipulations, obsolete survival skills—the parts of us that make us cringe with embarrassment and shame. Conversely, we may be in denial about these not-so-hot parts of us. Eventually, transformative work requires willingness to acknowledge each of these character defects. Part of the process is consciously choosing to ask God to remove them. Sometimes these areas of concern are not so much defects as they are false beliefs, bad attitudes, and barriers to becoming all that we were created to be. Have you ever known someone that is so negative that you can see a dark cloud of doom floating above them? Everywhere they go, there are reasons not to believe, not to trust, not to delight. A negative person might have trouble identifying that as a defect of character—they might call it being realistic! Negativity is definitely a barrier to healthy and enjoyable relationship development. Anything that holds us back from living large and loving others has the potential for making the list of things that we need to be willing and entirely ready to ask God to remove.

Step 6: Making It Personal

1) In their book *One Day At A Time*, Mike and Julia Quarles say: "God is not trying to improve your old nature - He is giving you a new nature." [9] With this in mind, read Acts 3:19 in both *The Message* and NIV translations. Because you have been working the steps, reading scriptures, and preparing yourself to be entirely ready, God has been working to increase both your ability and willingness to change your mind. What are you ready to acknowledge you need to dedicate yourself to changing?

2) Read

> Ezekiel 36:35
> Galatians 1:5
> John 1:29
> Ephesians 1:7, 2:3-5
> Philippians 2:13 and 4:19
> Hebrews 9:11-15
> 1 John 3:4-6
> Hebrews 4:13-16 and 10:22
> 1 Peter 2:24

This is a lot to read, so it's okay to pick a couple of readings. What do these texts suggest is God's part in the process of removing our defects of character?

3) Read

       1 John 3:4-10

       Ephesians 2:3-5

       Ephesians 4:30-32

How might these texts help us to recognize a character defect?

4) If you are struggling with naming your particular character defects, read this list and see what jumps out at you.

Unhealthy dependencies on people, circumstances, things, etc.
Controlling and manipulating
Desperation
Fears
Anger
Negative, limiting beliefs
Worry
The need to understand
The need to blame
Waiting to be reasonably happy
The belief that we aren't responsible for ourselves
     and cannot take care of ourselves
Self-hatred
Lack of trust
Inappropriately placed trust
Addictions
Guilt
Shame
Inability to feel

Inability to deal appropriately with feelings
Fear of joy, love, commitment
Closed mind and/or heart
Attraction to the wrong people, things…
Need to be perfect
Need to fail
Past abuse and present abusing
Need to be a victim
Selfish, self-centered living
Inability to be empathetic
Need for chaos
Need for dysfunction
Limiting false beliefs about God, self, and others
Fear of intimacy
Failure to be our true selves
Other: _____

Write down any reasons you have for not desiring to have these self-limiting, self-defeating defects removed.

5) There are lots of reasons for wanting to change. Sometimes it is to please or impress others. At some point in our lives, most of us get in the mood to take on a "self-improvement" project. Usually these changes are temporary. If we try hard and no one is pleased or impressed or if our self-renovation gets to be too big a hassle, we go back to our comfortable patterns of living. I believe that lasting change—meaningful change—can take place. Transformation is most likely to occur when we are driven by an attitude of gratitude and a belief that we are changing for a purpose far larger than other people's opinions of us—or even our opinions of ourselves.

Read:
> Romans 12:1-4
> Ephesians 2:1-6
> Hebrews 4:13-16

These texts give us great news. We can be transformed. God wouldn't suggest we try anything that we cannot succeed at accomplishing under God's mighty power. Not only can we be transformed, we can know and do the will of God. That's incredible, but it's true. When you are ready, God will do for you what you cannot do for yourself—transform you from the inside out.

Write a declaration of your willingness to surrender to the transformation process.

6) Does the idea of transformation frighten you? Read Ephesians 3:12. If you ask God to transform you, you can know that it will be the most loving renovation project ever. God is not out to steal your identity; God is the one with the power to restore you to your best self!

I remember when I first became a believer, I thought that transformation would mean that everything about me would change (which reveals how broken and unworthy I saw myself). There was a particularly lovely lady in our church, and I thought I would become her. She is still the most gentle, kind, merciful, sweet person I know. Well, guess what? Transformation is not the same thing as a lobotomy. God made us, and he's asking us to become all he created us to be—not to become some idealized version of what we think a desperately devoted follower of God *should* look like. My friends will tell you that I have not become a replica of my spiritual mentor, but I am transforming. I'm becoming the real me.

Read:
> Isaiah 44:2a
> Psalm 139:16
> Ephesians 1:4a
> Psalm 139:15
> Isaiah 46:3-4
> James 1:18, 22-26

What in these texts suggests that God made the real you to be a gem of priceless value?

What are some assets that you can admit to as belonging to your true self?

Prayer

I think if you get to the point of being entirely ready, you'll know what to pray. I'm praying that you will be entirely ready, and you will call out to God—who eagerly desires to answer your prayers, provide you with wisdom, and grant you freedom!

Step 7

*We humbly asked him
to remove our shortcomings.*

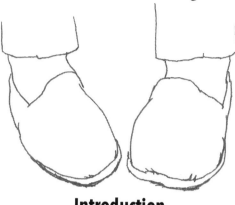

Introduction

I didn't grow up believing in shortcomings. In the 1970s and 1980s, for example, we were reading books like *I'm Okay, You're Okay*. In my psychology classes I studied theories about human development, and most of them seemed to indicate that my parents had done something to mess me up (which is a little incongruent with being okay). B. F. Skinner, a noted behavioral psychologist of the day, reportedly raised his kid in a box! The underlying belief was that we are born blank slates, and if people write on us carefully, we grow up into productive, reasonably happy humans. I was in my twenties, so I liked all these theories. I liked the idea that if someone found a shortcoming in me, it was someone else's fault— bad writing on the blank slate.

Then I grew up and birthed babies. Those theories didn't sound so great once I became a parental unit. I didn't birth a blank slate, in spite of my best intentions. We met our firstborn for the first time in the delivery room. Her dad, fearing that the bright lights of the operating room would hurt her newborn eyes, shielded her eyes with his hand as she gazed upward. She crinkled her forehead and studied us with rapt attention. We hadn't had a chance to whip out our chalk and write on her slate, but we soon discovered that this look was vintage Meredith. (I might also add that her dad has been busy "shielding" her from harm—as best he can— ever since our initial meeting.)

Our second-born also came mysteriously prewired. That kid slept all the time. He loved to sleep. Initially I thought it was because we gave him a pacifier. He gave up that pacifier years ago, but that young man still loves to sleep! He's just a laid-back kind of guy.

My third pregnancy was a challenge. I worried during the day because the baby never moved. I couldn't sleep at night because he kicked and carried on. He's all grown up now, and he is still a nocturnal creature. For his birthday he asked for a bike, so he can get more exercise—by riding his bike at night through the streets of Nashville! (You can imagine how, as a mother, I was tempted to include bubble wrap with the gift.)

Three kids with the same parents, and each child is very, very different. I'll bet you have stories like mine as well. Not only did the "blank slate" theory not pan out, but it wasn't long before the "born good only to be ruined by your parental units" theory also took a hit. Our kids weren't always good, and sometimes I couldn't find a way to blame myself or my spouse for their bad behaviors (I tried.) Maybe our family is different from yours, but we weren't okay all the time either. So we had three theories ditched: the "blank slate" theory, the "I'm okay, you're okay" theory, and the "it's always the parents' fault" theory.

Scripture puts a different spin on shortcomings. It eliminates the need to rationalize, justify, or shift blame. In Genesis, the first book of the Bible, it says: "…every inclination of his heart is evil from childhood" (Genesis 9:21). God says this is the nature of man. This is the same God who looked at the work of creation—mankind—and decided it was "very good." This is a paradox. We were pronounced "very good" by God himself, but we have a predisposition to live independently of God. Our problem at its core can best be defined as any time we live independently of God. We were created by God to live in an awesome, intimate relationship with God and with each other. But we have a predisposition to grow forgetful. We forget that there is a God and, more importantly, we forget that we are not God. As we forget God, we lose sight of how much we are loved. We grow insecure and look for love in all the wrong places. We also forget, or are never told, that we are born for a purpose, with a grand epic adventure set out before us by God. This leads us to look for meaning and significance in all the wrong places. Both of these by-products of forgetful living result in shortcomings. This is why we develop character defects. And here's the real kick in the pants: we, at birth, are vulnerable to wounding. So it's not okay to simply look around for someone to blame for our shortcomings. I have come to believe that it is less important for me to know how I developed these hurts, habits, and hangups than it is for me to simply acknowledge that they exist. As you've worked through these studies, that's exactly what has happened in steps 4, 5, and 6.

Step 7 is a really terrific one. We're asking God to do for us what we cannot do for ourselves: to remove our shortcomings. I love this verse: "For the eyes of the Lord range throughout the earth to strengthen those whose hearts are fully committed to him" (2 Chronicles 16:9, NIV). Think about it. Holy God is eagerly looking for us, but why? So that God can find the ones who aren't obeying and punish them for their decidedly not-okay ways? No. So that God can find out who is behaving well and pat them on the head? No. God is looking for someone, anyone, who is committed—so that he can strengthen us.

God wants to strengthen us. God who is all-knowing, eternal, king of kings and lord of lords, ruler of the universe and the unseen world, all-powerful, all-everything God wants to strengthen us. He wants to do an extreme makeover, because each of us needs one. We are not okay. We are not blank slates. We are humans. We are prone to wander and forget that there is a God—much less desire to follow hard after God. All we have to do is ask. Blessings to you as you continue on this awesome journey.

Key Terms

Humility: Humility is about being willing to be teachable, even in areas of our lives where we don't think we need instruction. Humility takes the "do not disturb" sign off of every single part of our personalities and invites God to be in charge. Humility asks: "How have I trusted in my own wisdom, strength, or wealth? Does my life exhibit the fruits of the Spirit (love, joy, peace, patience, kindness, goodness, gentleness, faithfulness and self control)? Am I able to discern the difference between healthy and unhealthy choices? Can I regularly choose to lay aside my natural instincts and old habits for a new and better way of living?"

Humility is not the same thing as humiliation, which means being embarrassed. False humility is when pride is cloaked with an "Oh, shucks…I'm just a nobody" response to a sincere word of affirmation. Real humility is when we can say thanks, and mean it, when someone points out something about us that is a reflection of God's transforming power. The kind of humility God teaches us about is the ability to see ourselves accurately—knowing the truth about ourselves—the good and the yet to be transformed!

Shortcoming: Shortcomings are anything in our lives that keep us from being our God-created selves. They are those traits that restrict and block our ever-increasing glory and the transformation process. One of my friends in recovery told a story that made an interesting distinction between a defect of character and a shortcoming. (I know not all people make this kind of distinction in the recovery world, but it has helped me so I will share it.) He says that a defect of character is like a pro baseball player who runs slowly. No matter what he does, he cannot run any faster; he's tried. He is great at lots of things—hitting and catching and throwing and sliding—but kind of below par in speed. That's a defect. But his shortcoming is this: the guy keeps trying to steal bases, even though his coach asks him not to. That's a shortcoming. He's not willing to accept his speed limitations. Notice in this story that because of all his marvelous qualities, he's still on the team. But he makes a better team player if he plays the game conscious of his limitations.

Ask: Asking God to remove our shortcomings acknowledges an important truth: God's got the power and we do not. Imagine going to speak to the most powerful person you know. Your intent is to ask that person for something huge, revolutionary, and life changing. How would you ask? Would you shout, complain, whine, or whimper? Would you doubt he or she could grant your request? Asking God is most appropriately done with respect and humility, believing that God indeed does have the power to grant our request.

Remove: The word remove suggests a gradual, healing, spiritual process of transformation. It is not instantaneous. This is not a step of struggle, but one of acceptance followed by responsibility. When we believe that God is in the business of transformation, we cooperate with the process. This process often comes with the pain of loss. The patterns of behavior which are being removed, although destructive and often deadly, have been with us for a long time. We have counted on them to produce predictable results. Sometimes this step leaves us filled with self-pity. But this step invites us to move past it. It reminds us of the consequences of our shortcomings and calls out to us to let go of the idolatry of self-defeating hurts, habits, and hangups. It calls us to run toward the light and toward our true, God-created identity.

Step 7: Making It Personal

1) In the past, you may have avoided looking at yourself honestly and avoided admitting the extent of your disabling behavior. Now is the time. The previous steps have prepared you well. Face your fear, and ask God to move you through the pain and toward the peace.

What do you fear about this transformation process?

2) Read:
> Psalm 25:4-5, 8-11
> Philippians 4:6

What encouragement do you find in these texts that might empower you to let the process continue?

3) Read: Acts 3:10. In the process of working steps 1-6 you have already seen some changes in your life—changes that may help guide you as the transformation process continues.

In what areas of your life have you already seen changes?

4) Read Matthew 23:12. Ask God to show you clearly what shortcomings you need to ask God to remove.

What shortcomings can you acknowledge in writing today?

5) Read:
> Hosea 4:6
> Obadiah 1:3

Ask God to reveal to you the issues in your life that would be improved if you would allow God to remove your shortcomings. What can you admit needs improvement in your life?

6) Read: 1 John 1:9.

Confession and forgiveness free us from the "strongholds" which hold us back. Keep this hopeful promise from 1 John in mind as you complete your seventh step. List aloud your defects of character, including resentments, self-centered defects that have harmed others, pride, lust, greed, perfectionism, etc. Be specific. What patterns do you notice? (Use this list when you pray the seventh-step prayer in the next section.)

Prayer

Here's a recommended prayer:

Dear Lord, I pray that I will hold nothing back from you.
I ask you to bring to my mind anything that I fear letting go of.
Remove this fear from my heart.
I give all of myself to you without reservation.
I want to be exactly and completely all that you created me to be.
I acknowledge that my defects of character hold me back from this pursuit.
I ask you now to remove from me every single defect of character that stands in the way of living out my true identity in you.
Help me let my old self die,
so that the new creation you intend for me to be might live.
Amen.

Step 8

*We made a list of all persons
we had harmed and became willing
to make amends to them all.*

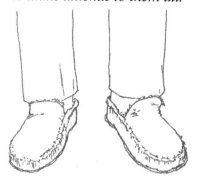

Introduction

Broken relationships usually result in some form of banishment, and banishment is a terrible thing. Either we avoid others, or they avoid us. If we do have contact, it is usually stilted and awkward. This is a form of banishment. If you study the lives of David, Absalom, and the rest of David's extended family (2 Samuel 14 is part of that saga), I believe you will discover that banishment happens simultaneously in both the seen and unseen worlds. Broken relationships with God have an impact on our ability to love others. And broken relationships with others have an impact on our ability to draw near to God.

We weren't created to cope well with banishment. We were created to carry within our hearts a huge capacity to receive and to give love. One of our primary purposes is to dispense this love with boundless enthusiasm and generosity of spirit. Life experiences may influence our thinking on this subject and cause us to doubt the veracity of this principle, but it is true. Anxiety, frustration, resentment, guilt, and shame are all emotions that can result from banishment; they are certainly an unwelcome part of life.

In 2 Samuel 14, we are reminded that God doesn't take away life. God doesn't put us in a self-protective bubble. Sometimes we allow ourselves to believe that once we become a follower of God, life should get easier. That would be awesome, but we just can't support that theory based upon scripture.

Although life may not get easier, it can get better. One of the ways God plans for us to have a more abundant life is by teaching us how to live with the messiness of life on planet earth. When we find ourselves in the midst of a broken relationship—banished in some way—God teaches us how to restore relationship. Subsequent steps will provide more details about that process. This step deals with getting real about the banishment.

In step 8 we're going to make a list of all the people we've harmed, and we're going to become willing to make amends to each and every one of them. I'm sure it is tempting to digress on this point and distract ourselves with thoughts of how others have offended us. Don't digress. Hang in with the process. The old adage, "nothing changes if nothing changes," is a great principle to apply right this minute. Previously, most of us have preferred to ruminate over the wrongs others have committed against us. Scripture turns us around, though, and points us in a different direction. Listen to how Jesus talks about this:

[Jesus says], "This is how I want you to conduct yourself in these matters. If you enter your place of worship and, about to make an offering, you suddenly remember a grudge a friend has against you, abandon your offering, leave immediately, go to this friend and make things right. Then and only then, come back and work things out with God. Or say you're out on the street and an old enemy accosts you. Don't lose a minute. Make the first move; make things right with him. After all, if you leave the first move to him, knowing his track record, you're likely to end up in court, maybe even jail." (Matthew 5:23-25, *The Message*)

If we're serious about trusting God, we've got to consider these instructions from God's son and how they might apply to our daily life experiences. Jesus is completely reliable. Take the step. Make the list.

Key Terms

List: Our task is to recall the names and faces of people we have harmed, write their names down, and consider how we've harmed them.

Became: Becoming is a process. If we will be responsible to God and make the list, God will help us become willing to make amends. How this happens is a deep mystery, and it takes place in the heart. Part of trusting God to do his part is simply making the list, in spite of our reluctance and our pain.

Willing: Willingness starts with accepting full responsibility for our own lives and for the harm we have done to others. The previous steps help prepare us for this willingness. Most of us have patterns of blaming others, avoiding responsibility, and seeking retribution for the wrongs done to us. Willingness means we make it our job to focus on our own behaviors and to stop distracting ourselves with the shortcomings of others.

Harm: Harm is caused physically (e.g. injuring or damaging persons or property, financial irresponsibility resulting in loss for another, refusing to abide by agreements legally made, neglecting or abusing those in our care), morally (inappropriate behavior regarding moral or ethical issues, including: fairness, doing the "right thing," irresponsible behaviors at home/work/etc., ignoring the needs of others or usurping the welfare of others with our own selfish pursuits, infidelity, abuse, lying, broken trust), or spiritually (failure to live out our God-created identity to the detriment of others; failure to support and encourage that same kind of living in others.) The root of harm is usually selfishness.

Amends: Amends is the process of sincerely seeking to repair the damage we have done. In his book, *Power to Choose*, Mike O'Neill describes this as a two-step process: apology and restitution.

Apology – "I was wrong." We tend to think of an apology as, "I am sorry." The problem with that sentence is its ambiguous nature. What are you sorry for? It can mean: "I'm a sorry no-good louse", "I'm sorry I got caught," "I'm sorry you're mad at me," or even "I'm sorry I have to deal with this." More drama doesn't make for a better apology. When we go to the shame-based "I'm sorry" place, sometimes we just fall all over ourselves and are willing to confess anything and everything for the sake of placating the person we have harmed. Making an apology isn't about confessing that which is not true. Humans make mistakes, and some of them are whoppers. Admitting this is good. But that is not the same as shame-based amends, which merely says, "Hey, I am a sorry person." A heartfelt apology will include a deeply remorseful expression of regret for harm done. Accepting responsibility for the wrong behavior is the heart of an effective apology and can be a humbling experience. Think of it like this: it takes more character and integrity to go to a person and tell them the exact nature of the wrong done than to grovel with an expression of regret that is ill-defined. Be specific.

Restitution – "What can I do to make this right?" Just saying we're sorry isn't enough, nor is it enough to decide for ourselves how to make things right. An apology without restitution is not amends. Sometimes restitution takes place before amends. If we owe back child support, pay it. If we can't make good on the full amount, then send what we can every month. Get real about what we can really afford. In situations where we fail to step up to the plate and live responsibly in the present moment, it is unlikely we will be given an opportunity to apologize. If we show some good-faith restitution, we may earn the right to be listened to. Remember to be willing to abandon all-or-nothing thinking. Perhaps we feel that the debt, financial or otherwise, is too large to repay. It is still important to ask the restitution question and proceed with restitution as best we can.

Step 8: Making It Personal

1) Read:
> 1 John 4:11-12
> Luke 6:27-31
> Ephesians 4:32
> Romans 15:1-3

As you prepare to make a list of all those you have harmed, consider the following categories: co-workers, strangers, enemies, family, friends, those you've neglected or abused, those you've harmed financially, those you've slandered or gossiped about or with, recipients of your rage, people with whom you acted out sexually, or people you used for self-seeking purposes.

Organize your list in the following three columns. Make the list.

Person or Relationship	Harm done	Impact on self and others

2) Read Luke 6:31. As God brings to mind those you have harmed, answer this question: "How would I feel, what would I think, and what would I do, if another person harmed me in the same way I caused harm in this situation?"

3) Check your list. Is it accurate and specific? Read Mark 11:25. Is there anyone you're deliberately avoiding putting on the list? Sometimes we believe that another's offense is so great against us that our offense against them is justified. This is the same kind of "stinking thinking" that leads to unremitting hurts, habits, and hangups. Go back and fix that list. Spend time in your group discussing why it's so hard to admit the harm done to certain people, and allow God to use the group to help you break out of old patterns of denial, blame shifting, and self-justification.

Prayer

One way to start praying over this step:

Lord, I ask you to help me make a list of all those I have harmed.
I confess that I have made decisions motivated
by selfishness and self-seeking.
This self-seeking has caused harm to others.
There are some people I have harmed who have also harmed me.
In these cases it is difficult for me to take responsibility
for my part of the problem.
I really need your help with these situations, Lord.
Free me from my reluctance to look at myself and my choices honestly.
In my fear, help me to remember that
any offense committed against another is an offense committed against
you.
Help me be brutally honest with myself
about not only my overt offenses, but the offenses of omission as well.
In my self-focused living there are many times
when my body has been present but my mind and spirit
have been distracted by my own obsessive thoughts of self.
Thank you that you make me
both willing and able
to proceed with this step.
Amen.

Step 9

*We made direct amends to such people
wherever possible, except when
to do so would injure them or others.*

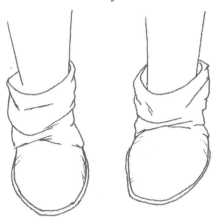

Introduction

As a pastor, I am often privileged to hear people's stories. Many of them are tales of broken hearts. Most of them involve offensive behaviors and broken relationships. Often the one wish people express to me is a simple one: forgiveness. They want to be able to extend forgiveness to those who have harmed them. And they want to be able to receive forgiveness from those whom they have harmed. I have heard the same story from countless young men and women: Someone has violated their trust. More than the act of violation of trust itself (which is serious enough), the fallout for individuals, families, and communities who do not have a process or skill sets to deal with offensive behavior appropriately continues to heap insult on injury. In my experience, an offended person often desires to hear from his or her offender. They want the offender to acknowledge wrongdoing. But if an offender doesn't approach the amends process properly, more harm is done. Step 9 offers valuable guidance for amend making.

If we were created to live and love, then it seems to me that our souls must be damaged by any broken relationship. We long for reconciliation, even if we don't understand this need. Our spirits long to be given the opportunity to forgive. Forgiveness doesn't mean that we just forget the offense and resume life as if nothing happened. Forgiveness doesn't require us to put ourselves in dangerous situations with dangerous people.

Forgiveness says that we are willing to transfer this case to a higher court—the holy court of God. In transferring it to God's court, we are asking God to do what he sees fit with the offense.

An effective step 9 is one step in the process of transferring the case to its proper jurisdiction. We ask for forgiveness, and we seek to make restitution. Sometimes we are forgiven and can make restitution; sometimes we are not forgiven, and our efforts to make restitution are rebuffed. Either way, when we offer to make amends, we are doing our part in the process of restoration.

I hope and pray that we will give people whom we have offended the opportunity to give us the gift of forgiveness. It is a burden to carry around that unopened package in our hearts. Hasn't our offense caused enough pain? Trust God. As we take responsibility for our part, we must allow God to take responsibility for the outcome.

Key Terms

Made: In step 4 we took a good hard look at ourselves and made a list that included people we have harmed, resentments we carry, and even patterns of behavior that continue to cause harm to self and others. Referring back to that list helped us make our step 8 list of people we have harmed. The ninth step requires that we do something with that list. Step 9 requires action.

Direct amends: The best amends is face to face. Sometimes a letter or a phone call is the next best thing. Ask God to give you the discernment necessary to decide how to approach the person you have harmed. However you choose to do an offer of amends, think about the other person's perspective. Don't startle them. Ask their permission to have a meeting. Accommodate them: meet in a place and at a time that is comfortable for them. Be considerate. Be aware that you were in the wrong, and the least you can do is make this situation as comfortable for them as possible. An indirect amends is appropriate for someone who is deceased or is otherwise inaccessible. Letters that are unmailed, prayers to God, or changes in behavior are all acceptable ways to make an indirect amends. Don't forget to make an amends to yourself—often you are the person you have harmed the most.

Wherever possible: Sometimes it is not possible to make a direct amends. I have a friend who committed adultery with her best friend's husband. She felt that a direct amends was not appropriate (her friend was not aware of the affair). She wanted to clear her conscience with her friend, but she felt that to do so might cause more harm. One way she chose to make restitution was to decide that she would never repeat this behavior in the future; she would compromise no more families with her bad behavior. She did make direct amends both to her husband, who did know about the affair, and to the man with whom she had the affair. She eased out of the friendship with her best friend at her husband's request. It took time and creativity to accomplish this without causing more problems with her friend. This is how amends was lived out in this particular situation. Some things were not possible to make right without causing more harm, but she made right what she could.

Injure: An ill-conceived step 9 can cause additional harm. It is important to pay attention to be sure that our motivation is not to make ourselves feel better. The only purpose for step 9 is to right previous wrongs— our previous wrongs. If we have resentments toward the individual we harmed, it might be best to delay the process. We may need to seek counsel. We don't want to let this beautiful step become just an opportunity to vent about our resentments, which could easily cause further injury. Admitting our wrong is not easy. We can think of a million excuses to avoid this step. Timing is important. Pray about this and seek God's counsel. We need to make sure that if we are hesitant to make an amends it is because of the potential harm to another person and not just because of our fears. I cannot count the number of adult children from dysfunctional families who have said to me: "If my mom or dad had only said they were sorry, I could get past this." Never underestimate the healing power of an effective amends. There may be people in our lives just waiting to hand us the beautiful gift of forgiveness—if we will but ask—and ask with a sincere heart.

Step 9: Making It Personal

1) Read:
> 1 John 4:19-21
> Matthew 5:23-24, 43-44
> Romans 13:8
> Philippians 2:3-4
> Matthew 18:21-28

Take time through prayer and meditation to do a thorough attitude check. Are the qualities listed in these texts true of you?

Ask yourself about each amends on your list:

Do I have a loving and forgiving attitude in this process?
Can I make my amends without blaming the other person in any way—even if there is plenty of blame to go around?
Am I focused only on my part, not theirs?
Am I willing to take full responsibility for my part?
Have I given up any expectation of a specific response from this person?
Can I trust that God will guide me through this process, no matter what the outcome?
Do I need to delay this process and do some additional step 4 work because of continued resentment or fear?

2) Read:
>   Proverbs 14:9
>   2 Timothy 1:7

Consider how your fear might be impeding your willingness to make direct amends.

Are your fears leading to excuses for avoiding this step?

3) Read Romans 13:7-8. Review the list you made in step 8. If needed, add to the list as God leads. Plan an appropriate amends: a phone call, a letter, or a face-to-face meeting. Make a list of the ones you think you should do first:

4) Read Philippians 2:1-4. Write a brief script of what you might say at the beginning of an offer of amends. It might include an expression of your desire to make amends and ask permission to make an amends. You could say something like, "I am working through some steps that are intended to help me. Part of that process has really convinced me that I have harmed you, and I would like to make an amends to you. Would you be willing to meet with me for that purpose?" Put this into your own words:

5) Read:

     Isaiah 50:7-8
     2 Timothy 1:7

Make an amends. Every ninth step has a first amends. If you have not done one yet, this is the time. What in these two texts might give you strength as you make an amends?

6) Read:
> Philippians 1:9-10
> 1 Peter 3:13

Having completed an amends, what was the outcome? If it was a totally positive experience for you, that's great. If the outcome was a disaster for you, remember that you still did what needed to be done and you have had a powerful reminder of the fact that we don't make amends so that we will "feel good." Other people's inability to respond appropriately is not information about us. The Philippians text talks about the value of increased knowledge and depth of insight. Whether the outcome of your amends felt good or bad, what increased "knowledge and depth of insight" did you gain from this experience?

7) Read:
> Ezekiel 33:15-16
> Luke 6:35-36
> Romans 8:1

Take note of how you feel when you have completed an amends. Are you experiencing more freedom? Do you have some increased motivation to continue this honest and humble lifestyle? Pay attention to the positive outcomes, and recognize the cause and effect of a sincere amends. (This is great encouragement for later, when you will inevitably have the opportunity to do this again.)

Prayer

Here's a prayer starter:

Lord, guide me through this process,
so I can make my amends with the right attitude.
Thank you for your merciful gentleness during this painful process.
I ask you to guide me every step of the way.
I realize that this step could be used by Satan
to undermine my healing process.
Protect me from the lies of the evil one.
Help me see myself as you see me—holy and dearly loved.
I know Christ died for me, and in so doing,
He already paid the ultimate price for my shortcomings.
Help me recall this truth as I make right in the seen world
what you have already made right in the unseen world.
I know that in some cases I cannot go back
and right the wrong I have done. I
f this is the case, reveal to me how I can change my behavior
in the future to reflect my intent to make restitution for my past misdeeds.
Thank you for the guidance and the power
you will provide for me
as I do what is pleasing to you
in this step.
Amen.

Step 10

We continued to take personal inventory,
and when we were wrong, promptly admitted it.

Introduction

Steps 4 through 9 provided us with a way to clean up the messes of our past. But the truth is that messes will still happen. Step 10 mercifully provides us with a way to deal with them as they occur. This is a huge blessing. Listen to what the *Big Book of Alcoholics Anonymous* says about step 10:

This thought brings us to step 10, which suggests we continue to take personal inventory and continue to set right any new mistakes as we go along. We vigorously commenced this way of living as we cleaned up the past. We have entered the world of the Spirit. Our next function is to grow in understanding and effectiveness. This is not an overnight matter. It should continue for our lifetime. Continue to watch for selfishness, dishonesty, resentment, and fear. When these crop up we ask God at once to remove them. We discuss them with someone immediately and make amends quickly if we have harmed anyone. Then we resolutely turn our thoughts to someone we can help. Love and tolerance of others is our code.[10]

Isn't this great? We now have an opportunity to practice these newly discovered skill sets, which is crucial if we want to live the abundant life that Christ has promised us.

When my children were small, they received inoculations against certain diseases. The shots were preventative medicine. Sure, they stung a little, but none of my kids have had polio, measles, mumps, rubella, or any of the other nasty diseases that felled so many children before the inoculations became available.

Step 10 is preventative medicine. It keeps us from falling back into the insanity, unmanageability, and dependencies that controlled us before we worked the twelve steps. Sure, it stings a little, but it can prevent the outbreak of a really bad disease. Recovery is a lifelong process—not something to turn on and off at our convenience.

These steps, when we apply them properly, are awesome. I'm reminded of 2 Timothy 3:16:

"There's nothing like the written Word of God for showing you the way to salvation through faith in Christ Jesus. Every part of Scripture is God-breathed and useful one way or another—showing us truth, exposing our rebellion, correcting our mistakes, training us to live God's way. Through the Word we are put together and shaped up for the tasks God has for us."

I believe the 12 steps are particularly effective at helping us make this passage of scripture a reality in our daily lives. As we are able to experience this transformation process, our lives can become really awesome. But our natural inclination to forget God and our human proclivity to think "it's all about me" can cause us to get sloppy with our recovery tools.

My husband has one teeny, tiny flaw that I'm sure he won't mind if I share with you. He's not that great at putting tools away. I discovered this one spring day when our kids were young. He repaired one of their bikes and stuck the screwdriver he used in a nearby flowerpot. He promptly forgot that it was there. I think that screwdriver stayed in that planter for months. One day our youngest child overheard me asking Pete where our screwdriver was. Michael said, "Mommy, they're growing out back in their special pot." Yes, my son believed that screwdrivers grew in pots. We can sometimes be like Pete, and get careless with our tools. We can forget them, toss them aside, and very subtly return to our old tried and true ways of dealing with life. Step 10 is a beautiful reminder not to get complacent.

Key Terms

Continued: People who keep track of these things tell us that most people who go on diets eventually gain their weight back. Experts tell us that this happens because people treat a diet like it is a temporary way of eating—something to be *on* or *off*. These same experts have studied people who have successfully lost weight and maintained their weight loss, and these are folks who choose to change their lifestyles. They make changes in how they eat every day. Step 10 helps us become successful at recovery. But it's not a diet; it is a lifestyle.

A tenth-step inventory is continual. We're monitoring ourselves during the day. When I am aware of feeling anxious or resentful, that awareness triggers my need to take inventory. I pause to prepare. I use the skills I have learned in steps four through nine, and I process through them quickly. At the end of the day, I do another inventory. I pause to reflect upon my day. Is there anything that is unresolved? Any leftover issues that can be resolved using my 12-step tools? In addition to this regular, daily step work it can be helpful to occasionally set aside a longer period of time to make sure that we've inventoried all our "stuff." I like to do this between Christmas and New Year's. If that season is too hectic, I do it the first week in January. I also try to take a day or two in mid-July. This just keeps the closets of my mind cleaned out. I've grown to enjoy these times of refreshment.

Take personal inventory: (You may want to review the step 4 study guide for a more detailed description of this process.) As I've continued to take inventory, I have found that God is always revealing to me new areas of potential growth. God is in the business of transforming us into our God-created selves. Over time, our inventories will change (this isn't a rehash of the past—steps 4 through 9 took care of that). For example, years ago I struggled with honesty. I got into the habit of not being honest in my dealings with my parents and it became a habit. I asked God to remove that character defect years ago. I cooperated with the process, and honesty issues don't pop up as often in my current inventories. But as I've matured, issues are brought to my attention that I wouldn't have even known were points of concern ten years ago. Currently I am asking God to remove a similar-but-different defect of character. As I've worked my program, my eyes are opened to new and different shortcomings that I need removed. I realize now that I'm not very honest with myself. I may no longer habitually tell half truths and whole lies to other people, but I definitely am prone to self-deceit. I'm not sure if I would have learned this about myself had I not continued to work the steps.

Wrong: As we mature, we become people who can admit when we are wrong. That's a struggle for most of us. One of the roadblocks to admitting that we're wrong is our strongly held convictions regarding what we perceive we're right about. Sometimes we fail to find solutions because we can't get off the question of whether we are right or not. My mother used to tell me that two wrongs don't make a right. That's true. Here's another way to look at it: one right doesn't cancel out one wrong. This isn't math class. You can be right about a million facts, but if you have wronged another in any way, you're still wrong. Fortunately, we now have skill sets to deal with wrongdoing. Neil Anderson has a phrase I love: "If you're right you don't need an excuse, if you're wrong you don't have an excuse." When we're wrong, let's just admit it, move past our denial, and continue the transformation process. Don't get stuck by the desire to be right!

Promptly: My experience has been that the more promptly I deal with an issue of wrongdoing, the better the outcome for all concerned. If I'm in the wrong in one area of my life, it seems to bleed over into other areas. When we're wrong and dragging our feet about making restitution, we find ourselves more defensive, easily offended, and just plain miserable. This results in more stuff to inventory. Pause to prepare, but don't procrastinate. Promptly admit we're wrong, and then we'll be free to move on.

Admitted it: This continues to be a vital part of the recovery process. Secrets aren't healthy. Admit our mistakes to self, to God, and to another individual (step 5). Now you're ready to take this admission and use steps 6, 7, 8, and 9 to resolve it. Here are two quotes that have helped me remember the importance of admitting things:

"Those who avert their eyes from evil commit the worst of sins." [11]

"It is not their sins per se that characterize evil people, rather it is the subtlety and persistence and consistency of their sins. This is because the central defect of the evil is not the sin, but the refusal to acknowledge it." [12]

Is it hard to admit when we are wrong, because we fear exposure of our failure. It is difficult for us to remember that our own personal hurts, habits, and hangups provide us with an opportunity to achieve incredibly awesome successes. A few months ago I spoke on failure. As I researched the topic, I came to realize that failure isn't what hinders success. Many "greats" in history have an impressive list of famous failures. But they didn't let their failures stop them. I list below some of these stories with the hope that they will encourage you to see your personal failures as opportunities to learn and ultimately experience the blessing of success as you grow into your true God-created identity.

Inspirational Famous "Failures" of the 20th Century [13]

Two brothers, both high school drop outs…Orville and Wilbur Wright.

"a sickly, delicate boy"…"he overcame severe asthma through strenuous exercise and eventually excelled at sports," who was this man? Theodore Roosevelt

Flunked elementary math, dropped out of school, worked for years as an obscure Swiss patent clerk, had trouble connecting to people. Albert Einstein

"to paint in such a way was as bad as drinking petrol in the hope of spitting fire"…criticism of who? Pablo Picasso

"I was convinced he was raving mad…such music would certainly cause a scandal." Conductor Pierre Monteux, on Igor Stravinsky's Rite of Spring

He spent his youth in poverty, singing for coins in saloons. His education was minimal and his musical training nonexistent…Irving Berlin

This man toiled for 20 fruitless years in the quest of a drug that would stop infections in humans. Who? Alexander Fleming, Discoverer of penicillin

"Box office poison" claimed one trade magazine…Katharine Hepburn

"You're not meant for show business. Go home." Said to…Lucille Ball

It may be difficult to remember, but the truth is that "I can do everything through him who gives me strength" (Philippians 4:13 NIV).

Step 10: Making It Personal

1) Read:
> Proverbs 14:29-30
> Romans 12:13
> 1 Corinthians 10:12
> Psalm 34:12-14

Are you being vigilant in your recovery journey? Sometimes we get complacent in our recovery and slip back into old self-defeating ways of living. If we don't live intentionally, we may find ourselves unintentionally back in the old, unhealthy patterns that led to unmanageability, dependency, and insanity. Are you aware of any old hurts, habits and hangups that are creeping back into your life? What are they? Make a list.

2) Read:
> Luke 4:18-19
> Job 33:33
> Psalm 32:1-7
> Psalm 139:23-25
> Isaiah 40:29
> Lamentations 3:19-33

Whew! That's a lot to read. If you've made it this far in the twelve-step process, you have experienced some of the same things described in these scriptures. Take some time and write out all the blessings you have experienced as a result of your twelve-step journey. Ask God to reveal blessings that you haven't previously recognized.

3) Read:

      Ezekiel 36:26-27, 31
      John 8:3-11
      Romans 8
      2 Corinthians 5:17 and 7:10
      James 1:23-25
      2 Peter 1:3-11

What good news do you find in each of these scriptures? Record them so that you can remind yourself of the gentleness with which God responds to us and the provisions he makes for us.

4) Read:

      Genesis 4:2-7
      Isaiah 29:15-16
      Hebrews 4:12-13

Notice in the text from Genesis that God knew more about Cain than Cain was willing to acknowledge about himself. The other texts emphasize that nothing is hidden from God's sight. After you prayerfully ponder this, review the material in step 4 and continue taking a searching and fearless moral inventory. List any areas of your fourth step work that might need an update.

5) When we did our fourth-step inventory, we were cleaning up a lot of baggage from the past. If we did a thorough and effective fourth step, a regular tenth step will probably be a lot shorter. On the other hand, sometimes a tenth-step inventory helps us see things from a different perspective and we find new areas that need some serious inventory work.

Take a look at:
    1 Corinthians 13
    Matthew 6:24 and 7:20-23
    Luke 6:27-28
    Galatians 5:13-15 and 6:3-5
    Ephesians 4:17-25; 5:15-16
    Colossians 3:5-8

Use these passages as meditative guides and see if you find new reasons to do inventory or new areas of your life that could benefit from a regular inventory and 'admission.'

6) Just as was the case in our fourth-step inventory, it is always tempting in our more regular tenth-step work to become distracted by the failings, shortcomings, and character defects of other people. It always seems just a little bit easier to do other people's inventory than to do our own. If we practice regular inventory, however, we begin to see others in a new light. The authors of *The Twelve Steps for Christians* talk about it this way:

"We experience a release from resentment when we begin to understand that those who mistreated us were also spiritually sick. We extend to them the tolerance and forgiveness that God gives us. When we concentrate on our own inventories in Steps Four and Ten, we put the wrongs of others out of our mind, and we focus on our faults, not the faults of others." [14]

This point is also emphasized in the *Big Book of Alcoholics Anonymous*:

"We realized that the people who wronged us were perhaps spiritually sick. Though we did not like their symptoms and the way these disturbed us, they, like ourselves, were sick too. We asked God to help us show them the same tolerance, pity, and patience that we would cheerfully grant a sick friend. When a person offended we said to ourselves, 'This is a sick man. How can I be helpful to him? God save me from being angry. Thy will be done." [15]

Here's a self-assessment quiz adapted from *The Twelve Steps for Christians* [16]. Make an assessment of yourself on a scale of one to ten (one=you're practically Mother Teresa; ten =you could have gotten a part in the movie Anger Management) with respect to each of the following markers of changed attitudes toward others:

I feel increased tolerance for others
I am able to forgive those who hurt me
I am able to focus on my own inventory
I am able to release the need to retaliate
I can accept appropriate responsibility
I can able to feel compassion for others

7) I have a therapist friend who often reminds me that compulsions are ways we try to cope with our unmanageable lives. He says we suffer from "maladaptive coping skills." This is a fancy way of saying that many of us have trouble dealing with our feelings in a healthy manner. For many, fear is an unmanageable emotion. Working a spiritual recovery program can inspire us to experience fear differently. Inspired by a new way of "seeing," we find that we can recover from our "maladaptive coping skills."

The authors of *The Twelve Steps for Christians* put it this way:

Fear becomes less of a problem for us as our faith in God grows. We list our fears one by one and consider why they have power over us. We especially note the fears that grow out of our failed self-reliance. God is able to manage where we could not. Our faith empowers us to release our need for self-reliance and the fear that goes with it." [17]

Here is another self-assessment exercise adapted from *The Twelve Steps for Christians*. Evaluate yourself on a scale of one to ten (one=no fear; ten=very, very afraid).

I feel less threatened
I find myself more able to embrace change
I can face my fear honestly
I am growing in my ability to rely on God
I feel more joy
I pray more

Prayer

I do not always have words for my prayers. On days when I cannot find the words but want some, I turn to scripture for inspiration. How about speaking this ancient and well-know scripture passage as a prayer today?

The Lord is my shepherd.
I lack nothing.
He lets me rest in grassy meadows;
he leads me to restful waters;
he keeps me alive.
He guides me in proper paths
for the sake of his good name.
Even when I walk through the darkest valley,
I fear no danger because you are with me.
Your rod and your staff—
they protect me.
You set a table for me
right in front of my enemies.
You bathe my head in oil;
my cup is so full it spills over!
Yes, goodness and faithful love
will pursue me all the days of my life,
and I will live in the Lord's house
as long as I live. (Psalm 23, CEB)

Step 11

*We sought through prayer and meditation
to improve our conscious contact with God,
praying only for knowledge of his will
for us and the power to carry it out.*

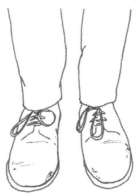

Introduction

"This book of the law shall not depart from your mouth, but you shall meditate on it day and night, so that you may be careful to do according to all that is in it; for then you will make your way prosperous, and then you will have success." (Joshua 1:8 NASB)

I wish I could honestly tell you that I embrace this perspective joyfully, but that would be deceitful. Some days, the woes of the world perch heavily on my shoulders, pushing me down into a lethargic pit of quiet and desperate apathy. On those days I am more drawn to solitaire than prayer and meditation. I find all sorts of reasons to not pray. Since I'm a pastor, this tendency to zone out rather than focus on my conscious contact with God is embarrassing. But working a recovery program has taught me that vigorous honesty is essential. So there it is—I struggle to pray, even as I know that prayer and meditation is a key element of any spiritual program of recovery.

In recovery, I've also learned that the next right step doesn't require enthusiasm. Commitment to the 12-step journey is a daily expression of a lifelong process. It is a lifestyle. The eleventh step provides me with structure when my sincerity isn't enough to get me moving in a healthy direction. I am comforted when I realize that I am not alone in my resistance to receiving comfort from conscious contact with God. The psalmist certainly understood this when he wrote the following psalm:

I lie in the dust, completely discouraged; revive me by your word. I told you my plans, and you answered. Now teach me your principles. Help me understand the meaning of your commandments, and I will meditate on your wonderful miracles. I weep with grief; encourage me by your word. Keep me from lying to myself; give me the privilege of knowing your law. I have chosen to be faithful; I have determined to live by your laws. I cling to your decrees. Lord, don't let me be put to shame! If you will help me, I will run to follow your commands. (Psalm 119:25-32 NLT)

No matter what season we find ourselves in, God is always in the mood to draw near to us. We don't have to be perky, perfect, and performance-driven in our pursuit of God. Even when we are broken, battered, and beaten down, God is available to us.

I don't know where you are today in your spiritual journey. Perhaps this is a good day and all is right with your world. I hope so. But if it is not, and if you are completely discouraged, weeping with grief, lying to yourself, faithless, and far, far away from God, know this: it is still a good day to practice the eleventh step.

Key Terms

Sought: Healthy relationships are like two-way streets. Two-way streets work because everybody follows the rules: driving on the correct side of the road, not crossing the yellow line, etc. Scripture is clear. God desires and seeks relationship with his children. Healthy relationships stay healthy when we follow the guidelines. God created us, and he knows how to relate to us. All good relationships are mutually satisfying. There is healthy give and take within those relationships. Step 11 guides us in the process of building an intimate relationship with God.

Prayer: Prayer is speaking with God. When we follow the disciplines of the 12 steps, we learn that prayer includes two essential elements. First, it includes an admission of our powerlessness (step 1). Second, it includes an acknowledgment of our daily choice to accept God as our higher power (step 2). Furthermore, the insights we have gained in this process will drive a large part of our continued prayer by asking God to remove our shortcomings, etc.

Meditation: Meditation is listening to God. Some believers are scared off by the term *meditation*, but do not fear! Meditation is a biblical concept.

My meditation of Him shall be sweet; I will be glad in the Lord. Psalm 104:34)

I love Mike O'Neill's personal description of contemplative prayer:

> "Let your body relax, and let all the tension and all the thoughts go out, and all the preoccupations. Either meditate on a small scripture or meditate on just one or two words. I meditate on Jesus, the Holy Spirit, or Abba Father (Romans 8:15). My mind will wander now and then, but I just return to my beginning meditation and try to love God." [18]

Improve our conscious contact with God: Many voices compete for our attention: our culture, our family of origin, our false beliefs, and even the thoughts that spring up as a result of our tendency to live self-centered and self-seeking lives. Improving our conscious contact with God confronts the voices that seek to distract us from our God-created identity and purpose. We must replace the voices that historically have led us to unintentional, counterproductive behaviors. Nothing changes if nothing changes.

The conscious contact we seek here is far greater than a mere acknowledgement that God exists. It is about relationship. Relationships take work. I've been married for over 30 years. I know a lot about my husband, but every day, we make an effort to maintain conscious contact. My husband travels several days a week. At the end of every day and sometimes several times during the day, we talk. We take turns. One talks, the other listens. Some nights, one of us is more chatty than the other. But in the end, I think it evens out (he might disagree) because both of us are highly committed to a satisfying love relationship. If we didn't do this, we would lose our intimate connection. Relating to God is no different. We talk. We pray. And God listens. God talks and we listen—that's meditation.

Knowledge of his will: My husband grew up in a home of believers. I did not. I always thought that in our marriage he would be the one who had the knowledge of God's will, and I'd have to rely on him to get it straight and explain it to me. I didn't believe that I'd be able to learn enough to acquire a working knowledge of God's will, much less acquire the power to carry it out. I was wrong. Read Romans 12:1-2. This scripture applies to all of us. We can come to know and do God's good, pleasing, and perfect will. God desires this for us. Often God wants this more for us than we desire it for ourselves. Don't let our old false beliefs shaped by shame and self-loathing keep us from celebrating this point: God wants us to know his will, and he desires to empower us to carry it out (Philippians 2:13). Isn't that incredible? Sometimes we wonder what we should pray. When in doubt, the eleventh step prayer for the knowledge of God's will and the power to carry it out is a surefire guarantee. It is completely within the will of God and within God's power to answer it. God is not fickle. God will hear and answer our prayer. But I must admit that I have spent many an hour asking for God's will, meaning that I desire to know what God wants me to do. Recently I've come to appreciate that God tells me that my work is to believe (John 6:29). Knowledge of God's will is not just about what I "do", but perhaps more about who I "be." This has led me to conclude that God's will is always for me to know God better. So daily I seek to know God. I've found that when I am aware of God's heart, my heart seems quite capable of figuring out what God wants me to do.

Power to carry it out: I don't want to mislead anyone. Coming to know God isn't an act of passivity. Knowledge informs our action. God has a plan and a purpose for us that involves action. But it is God's plan, God's power, and God's resources that will enable us to accomplish God's purposes. The scriptures point to the power of God and to God's desire to empower each of us. But make no mistake—it is God's mission that we become aware of and choose to join. God chooses the assignment, not us. The awesome part of this process is that we can know that, ultimately, whatever God chooses for us is far more fulfilling than any plans we can think of for ourselves.

Step 11: Making It Personal

1) Read:
>Philippians 2:13
>Romans 12:1-3
>Ephesians 1:11

God is at work. Sometimes we forget this awesome truth. Think about how you have seen God at work in your life. Ask God to reveal to you times when you've failed to recognize and appreciate God's provision. Using your creativity, find a way to express gratitude. Take a minute to write a short prayer of gratitude to God.

2) Cause and effect is an important principle that we sometimes fail to appreciate. Read:
>Joshua 1:8
>Psalm 1:1-3
>Proverbs 3:5-7
>Isaiah 26:3-4
>Philippians 4:6-7

What is the cause-and-effect relationship that is consistently revealed in these passages?

3) Having made it this far in the twelve-step process, you have probably come to realize how many of your shortcomings have led to hardship. But have you considered the opposite point? How you live can indeed result in peace, success, and blessings! Write any thoughts you have about your experience of changed behavior leading to a more peaceful, successful, and blessed life:

4) Read:

2 Chronicles 16:9
Hosea 6:3
Psalm 25:4-5
Jeremiah 29:13-14
Matthew 7:7-8

When I began my intentional program of prayer and meditation, I worried that it wouldn't work. I'm not sure what I thought it would mean to have a spiritual program that "worked," but I believed that perhaps it wouldn't work for me. Many of us have had crushing disappointments. I don't suppose that it is all that surprising to wonder if God will deliver on promises made. Have you found a scripture passage during your step work that has stirred you? Meditate on this scripture daily. Ask God to reveal to you how promises made are being fulfilled. Record here what you learn.

5) Read Luke 6:12. Prior to His arrest, trial, crucifixion, and resurrection, Jesus went off by himself to pray. If Jesus himself needed to refresh his spirit in prayer, it's probably arrogant of us to presume we can live our lives without this kind of vital communication with God. Spend some time thinking about how to structure a regular time of prayer and meditation. Where can you set up a quiet place away from distractions? What time of day can you consistently meet with God? Can you be alert at this time? What "supplies" do you need—a Bible? A journal? Outline here the basic elements of your plan to increase your conscious contact with God:

Prayer

Dear Lord, I thank You for making me
both willing and able to do
your good, pleasing, and perfect will.
I thank you for the ability to have a sound mind—even the mind of Christ.
I thank you for peace of mind.
I thank you for your promise of freedom and the ability to know the truth.
I thank you that in this world I can always find someone
who is smarter, richer, wiser, stronger, and better than I,
but that you have consistently used the weak to manifest your strength.
Father God, I ask you to continue to sharpen my senses
so that I may grow in my awareness of you.
I pray for increased intimacy, Lord.
I want to know you better than anyone or anything.
I ask for the fulfillment of your promises in me
    that I may have the mind of Christ,
    that I may know your will,
    and that you will empower me to carry that will out in all of my affairs.
May your word dwell in me richly.
Amen.

Step 12

*Having had a spiritual awakening,
we tried to carry this message to others
and to practice these principles
in all our affairs.*

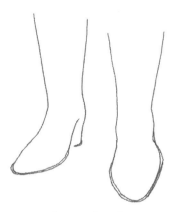

Introduction

"I just can't look at myself in the mirror anymore."
"I am not the person I thought I would be when I grew up."
"This isn't who I really am."
"Have you ever woken up in the morning, seen your reflection in the mirror, and not known who that person is staring back at you?"
"I am so ashamed."
"I don't know what has happened to me; I've lost myself. I'm a stranger to myself."

I hear these sentiments expressed by hurting people on a regular basis—heck, I feel this disconnect between the person I am today and the person I dream of becoming. Finding our way back to God ultimately leads to finding our way back to our true selves. It's a glorious, sacred, and sometimes secret truth, and the journey is uneven, filled with backtracks and rabbit trails. Recovery isn't a quick fix or a magic pill—but it can be an awesome life.

A passage of scripture that reminds me of my life's work is found in the book of Ephesians.

It's in Christ that we find out who we are and what we are living for. Long before we first heard of Christ and got our hopes up, he had his eye on us, had designs on us for glorious living, part of the overall purpose he is working out in everything and everyone. It's in Christ that you, once you heard the truth and believed it (this Message of your salvation), found yourselves home free—signed, sealed, and delivered by the Holy Spirit. This signet from God is the first installment on what's coming, a reminder that we'll get everything God has planned for us, a praising and glorious life. (Ephesians 1:11-14 *The Message*)

This praising and glorious life—this God who is in the business of working this purpose out in everything and everyone—is ours for the living. We can bring the message of hope to hurting people once we've lived it. Take a moment to prayerfully reflect. Once ashamed, without hope, and certainly helpless, we may have lost some things along the way that were important to us. We lost ourselves. Who we once were is gone, and a new creation lives. Once upon a time, we lost our confidence and our belief in ourselves and in God.

Sometimes I need a reminder of the possibilities that await me if I will surrender myself to God's care and control. When I get discouraged, I have a notebook with suggestions about how I have worked through this malaise in the past. Selections from Proverbs can also provide quick reminders of what the future holds for someone willing to do the work of recovery. For example:

Hear, for I will speak excellent and princely things; and the opening of my lips shall be for right things. For my mouth shall utter truth, and wrongdoing is detestable and loathsome to my lips. All the words of my mouth are righteous (upright and in right standing with God; one whose aim is true); there is nothing contrary to truth or crooked in them. (Proverbs 8:6-8 AMP)

Sometimes we fall down, but there is beauty in recognizing that both the fall and the return from disgrace are beautiful parts of our story. May God richly bless as we continue on this journey of faith. On those occasions when we notice that our performance isn't matching our potential, remember who it is that works in and through us—it never was about the performance. Remember the process of humbling self and hunting for God that led us to this point. As those who have gone before us, we fight the good fight. As we are responsible, God will never disappoint.

Key Terms

Spiritual awakening: A spiritual awakening is part of effective twelve-step work. I find that people who have spiritual awakenings possess the ability to see the world through what I like to call "God-vision goggles." Some people have dramatic moments of clarity. Others experience it as a process. Many say that it was in hindsight that they became aware of God's hand on their lives. For years, evangelicals have used the term "born again." Although many scorn this phrase, I think it clearly describes what happens—an awakening in our hearts to God. My spiritually awake friends all agree that it's an "a-ha" experience. It's hard to describe if you've never experienced it for yourself. (Read 1 Corinthians 2 for a better understanding as to why this is a tough concept to describe.)

As a result of these steps: If we choose to work these steps, then our life will be changed. It isn't the steps that change us. It is God who changes us. But these steps are a way to learn how to talk to God, to listen to God, and to respond to God. These steps have done more to help me learn what it means to be a kid of the King than anything else in my life experience. But I'm not foolish enough to believe it was the steps that saved me. It was God. The steps are a tool that God uses to get our attention.

Carry this message: In recovery communities there is a phrase that describes this message: the sharing of one's experience, strength, and hope. This isn't about giving someone information. Information can always be debated. Carrying the message is deeply personal. It is experiential. It cannot be refuted or denied. Others can legitimately say that they cannot relate to one's story. But each of us has a life story to share, and no one can take that away from us.

Others: Who are these others with whom we share? They are people that God brings into our lives. Together we discuss our experiences and hopefully our solutions. Scripture talks about this process in the book of 2 Corinthians:

Praise be to the God and Father of our Lord Jesus Christ, the Father of compassion and the God of all comfort, who comforts us in all our troubles, so that we can comfort those in any trouble with the comfort we ourselves have received from God. (2 Corinthians 1:3-4 NIV)

This is God's plan for ministry. It works like this. As we grow up in our spirituality, we begin to see ourselves more accurately and develop the discernment to see others with clarity of vision too. As we move through the growing up process, we develop life experience. Sometimes, by the grace of God, we meet people who are ready to hear a solution. When this happens, it is a God thing. Frankly, many people lose hope in solutions. They believe the lie that nothing will ever change. When scripture says that we are ambassadors for Christ, this is what that verse means. We have been sent to use our experience, strength, and hope to carry this good news to other hurting people. Often God puts people in our path with the exact same hurt that we have experienced. In Genesis (50:20), Joseph speaks of this miraculous working of God. He's been seriously mistreated in his life, but he learned through his own spiritual awakening how to rise above the obstacles and turn them into opportunities. When confronted by his former tormentors (his brothers), Joseph says this: "You intended to harm me, but God intended it for good to accomplish what is now being done, the saving of many lives." God is the ultimate recycler! He takes our pain and powerfully moves in and through us to bring good out of situations that are thoroughly evil. This process is thwarted if we haven't worked through our own pain. When we've begun to live out the solution, rather than wallow in the problem, we might find that we have changed—and the process may feel quite mysterious. People will want to know what happened to us.

Practice these principles in all our affairs: Unless and until these principles are applied to all areas of our lives, we will reduce our chances of effectively working a twelfth step. We can learn a lot of things and share a lot of information about the 12 steps, but we will not see much fruit from our labor. What does it mean to practice? Just what it says: every day, all the time, in every situation, we use what we've learned in these steps to order our thinking, our believing, and our behaving. There's an old saying that actions speak louder than words. I can't think of a more apt phrase to remind us of the importance of living what we try to share with others. (See Philippians 4:8-9.)

Obedience is a frightening concept to most of us. We have track records that clearly indicate that this is not our strong suit. But the skill set of obedience is crucial to thriving in the midst of the twelfth step. Oftentimes I have asked the Lord: "How can I obey that which I don't understand? How can I obey that which I understand and feel inadequate to carry out?" Here are some principles that I've learned from scripture that help me live out my own 12th step:

a) It is God who makes us both willing and able to fulfill his good purpose. (See Philippians 2:13 and 2 Corinthians 1:20-22).

b) We serve a God who is able and willing to transform us. God's plans cannot be thwarted. ("My purpose will stand, and I will do all that I please." See Isaiah 46:9-11.)

c) We've been given one instruction: to believe. When we take responsibility to believe, God assumes responsibility for the outcome. I can only assume that God is a big enough God to handle my predisposed shortcomings and defects of character. (Study John 6:29; Exodus 14:14; 2 Chronicles 16:9)

d) God has said he will equip us. Who am I to doubt? (Read 2 Timothy 3:16-17)

In our humanity, all these big plans are not immediately obvious to us. We are easily deceived and distracted, and we regularly deny the truth about our lives. Our work will require that we actively seek to live out in the open, with nothing hidden. Listen to how the Apostle Paul talks about this process:

Whenever anyone turns to the Lord, the veil is taken away. Now the Lord is the Spirit, and where the Spirit of the Lord is, there is freedom. And we, who with unveiled faces all reflect the Lord's glory, are being transformed into his likeness with ever-increasing glory, which comes from the Lord, who is the Spirit. 2 Corinthians 3:16-18 (NIV)

Recently I had cataracts removed, and let me tell you, there is a lot of cool stuff to see in this world. I see clearly and in full color for the first time in a long time, and it's awesome! We find the Lord in the unseen world. It is there that we meet God, and it is there that we find freedom. You were created to be free. This freedom cannot be bought, bartered, or begged for—only God provides freedom.

As Paul says, when we meet the Spirit of the Lord and find our freedom, we become a reflection of God's glory. This is a process; the transformation takes place in "ever-increasing glory." This glory is a bestowed glory, merely a reflection of the Lord's glory—a truth so profound that it eliminates any hint of arrogance or pride. It is a humbling glory, but glory indeed—a shining that draws others to us. We are now ready to carry God's message of hope to hurting people.

Step 12: Making It Personal

1) Read:

> Jude 20:23
> 2 Timothy 4:3-5
> 2 Corinthians 1:3-4
> Galatians 6:1-2
> 1 Peter 5:8-9
> Titus 3:3-7

Whom does God say we should serve? We've learned in our studies of this step that God sends people for us to serve who have experienced the same trials we have experienced. Write down your past hurts, habits, and hangups. Make a list of life experiences that have been painful. Refer to this list as a guide. In the areas of your pain, can you think of a person whom you have met that may have experience, strength, and hope to share with you?

2) Read:

> 2 Chronicles 25:8
> Psalm 27:1
> Acts 1:8
> 2 Timothy 1:7
> Ephesians 3:12
> 1 Thessalonians 5:16

Every spiritual being can have great confidence to serve. What do these passages teach you about serving?

3) Read:

> Proverbs 15:23, 25:11
> Matthew 10:7-8
> 2 Timothy 2:20-22
> 2 Corinthians 4:7

Do you see the hope in these texts? You can be effective! You can be a facilitator for hope, healing, and change! Perhaps you, like many others, have felt like you were ineffective, hopeless, and unusable in this world. That is simply not true. Consider long and hard the implications of these scriptures. Write down how these truths affect you.

4) God has told us that our service to others is beneficial not just for others but for us personally. Although this isn't the reason we serve, it certainly doesn't hurt to remember that God promises us these benefits.

Read:

> John 8:31-32
> John 15:7-8
> Matthew 10:32-33

What are some of these benefits that you can expect to receive if you serve the Lord?

5) We have learned from scripture that the work of every believer is this: to believe in the one whom God sent. Having done this, scripture offers lots of insights as to how to proceed from that point.

Read:

> John 15:15-17
> Ephesians 5:1-2
> I Peter 4:7-8, 19

Based on these texts, what do you think God considers the most important way we can demonstrate our believing in the one he has sent?

Prayer

Lord, I continue on this journey of spiritual awakening.
I am both encouraged and frightened
by this mandate to give to others
what you have so generously given to me.
Protect me from the lies of the evil one
who would attempt to shame me and discourage me
from sharing my experience, strength, and hope.
Protect me from my own self-centeredness.
Sometimes it's easier to judge others than it is to love them.
Remind me how others helped me.
I am so grateful for the help others have given me.
Thank you for the privilege of returning this grace
by sharing it with others.
Father, I ask for your continued guidance and wisdom.
I remember that apart from you I can do nothing.
But with you I can do all things!
Thank you, Lord.
Amen.

Afterword

You did it—with God helping you! Praise be to God! I thank God for your willingness to embark on this journey. I hope you take some time (maybe 10 minutes!) to dance and shout in exultation at your persistence. Most of us, having made this trip, come to believe that the 12 steps are life saving...and life giving. I would be remiss if I didn't share with you the perspective of most who take these steps: keep stepping. These steps are more like a daily practice than a good read or a temporary program. Because these steps are a practice, not a one-time study, we have developed more resources about the 12-step process. Three resources that I particularly want to call your attention to are:

1. Juanita Ryan has an amazing video series on *"Distorted Images of God"*. For those interested in continuing the journey of faithful living, this series provides some restorative structure to replace previously held, potentially abusive images of God that so many of us struggle with in our recovery.

2. Looking for expanded resources for some of the key terms that are essential for transformative recovery? Check out our videos on recovery and spirituality. We are continuing to add supplementary resources as companions to these videos.

3. Kim Engelmann and I have teamed up to provide both a book and workbook entitled, *"No More Running In Circles"*. This Bible study and 12 step compilation includes Kim's personal story and experience with recovery. It could be a small group study experience appropriate for church and recovery communities interested in productive suffering and transformational recovery.

These are all available at:

www.nacr.org

A Few Books I Love

It's very difficult to create a comprehensive recommended reading list, so this isn't one. Below are a few suggestions that have been helpful to me in my own recovery journey. Reading is one way that I continue to challenge my recovery muscles, and here are just a few classics that I return to regularly for spiritual exercise.

Addiction and Grace, by Gerald May
A Spiritual Kindergarten, by Dale and Juanita Ryan
Addictive Thinking & the Addictive Personality, Twerski & Nakken
Beyond Codependency, Melody Beattie
Boundaries, Henry Cloud and John Townsend
Breaking Free, Beth Moore
Bridges to Grace, Liz Swanson and Teresa McBean
Changes That Heal, Henry Cloud
Codependent No More, Melody Beattie
Daily in Christ, Neil T. Anderson
Distorted Images of God, by Dale and Juanita Ryan
Every Man's Battle, S. Arterburn & F. Stoeker
Every Young Man's Battle, S. Arterburn & F. Stoeker
Food Addiction, Kay Sheppard
Freedom From Addiction, Neil T. Anderson & Mike/Julia Quarles
He Restores My Soul, Marcy Hawkins (A Recovery Bible Study & 12 Step workbook)
Jesus, My Father, the CIA and Me, by Ian Morgan Cron
Keep Breathing, Juanita Ryan
Life Recovery Bible
Recover to Live, by Christopher Kennedy Lawford
Rooted In God's Love, Dale and Juanita Ryan
Soul Repair, Jeff VanVonderen, Dale and Juanita Ryan
The Awakened Heart, by Gerald May
The 12 Steps for Christians, RPI Publishing, Inc.
The Language of Letting Go, Melody Beattie
The Power to Choose, Mike O'Neill
The Story of God, The Story of Us, by Sean Gladding
Victory Over the Darkness, Neil T. Anderson

The 12 Steps

The 12 Steps of Alcoholics Anonymous uses the term "alcohol" in step 1. This adaptation makes a single change in the language of the steps: we use "our dependencies" instead of "alcohol." The original 12 steps are found in "Twelve Steps and Twelve Traditions" page 15, Copyright © 1952, 1953, 1981 by A.A. World Services®, Inc. All rights reserved.

Step 1. We admitted that we were powerless over our dependencies - that our life had become unmanageable.

Step 2. We came to believe that a power greater than ourselves could restore us to sanity.

Step 3. We made a decision to turn our life and will over to the care of God as we understood him.

Step 4. We made a searching and fearless moral inventory of ourselves.

Step 5. We admitted to God, to ourselves, and to another human being the exact nature of our wrongs.

Step 6. We were entirely ready to have God remove all these defects of character.

Step 7. We humbly asked him to remove our shortcomings.

Step 8. We made a list of all persons we had harmed and became willing to make amends to them all.

Step 9. We made direct amends to such people wherever possible, except when to do so would injure them or others.

Step 10. We continued to take personal inventory, and when we were wrong, promptly admitted it.

Step 11. We sought through prayer and meditation to improve our conscious contact with God, praying only for knowledge of his will for us and the power to carry it out.

Step 12. Having had a spiritual awakening as a result of the steps, we tried to carry this message to others and to practice these principles in all our affairs.

Footnotes

1] Hadley Cantril, *The Psychology of Social Movements* (Transaction Publishers, 2002), pp. 147-148.

2] Anon., *Alcoholics Anonymous Comes of Age* (New York: Alcoholics Anonymous World Services, Inc., 1957), p. 199.

3] This definition was prepared by the Joint Committee to Study the Definition and Criteria for the Diagnosis of Alcoholism of the National Council on Alcoholism and Drug Dependence and the American Society of Addiction Medicine and was approved by the Boards of Directors February 3, 1990 and February 25, 1990 respectively.

4] Abraham Twerski, *Addictive Thinking: Understanding Self-Deception* (Hazelden, 1997) p13

5] Neil Anderson, *Daily In Christ* (Harvest House Publishers , 2000) Entry for October 14th

6] Friends in Recovery, *The Twelve Steps for Christians* (RPI Publishing Inc., 1994) p. 71.

7] Mike S. O'Neill, *Power to Choose* (Sonlight Publishing, 1992) p. 72.

8] Corrie ten Boom, *The Hiding Place*, (Bantam Books, 1971), pp. 27-28.

9] Mike and Julia Quarles, *One Day At A Time*, (Regal Books, 2000) p. 184.

10] Anon., *The Big Book of Alcoholics Anonymous* (Alcoholics Anonymous World Services, Inc, 2002) p. 84.

11] Carl Goldberg, *Speaking With The Devil*, (Penguin Group, 1996), p. 2.

12] Scott Peck, *People of the Lie*, (New York: Simon & Schuster, 1983), p. 69.

13] All quotes excerpted from *People Who Shaped The Century*, by the Editors of Time-Life Books (Simon & Schuster, 1999)

14] Friends in Recovery, *The Twelve Steps for Christians* (RPI Publishing, Inc., 1994) p. 170-171.

15] Anon., *The Big Book of Alcoholics Anonymous* (Alcoholics Anonymous World Services, Inc, 2002) p. 66-67.

16] Friends in Recovery, *The Twelve Steps for Christians* (RPI Publishing Inc., 1994) p. 170-171.

17] Friends in Recovery, *The Twelve Steps for Christians* (RPI Publishing Inc., 1994) p. 170-171.

18] Mike S. O'Neill, *Power to Choose* (Sonlight Publishing, 1992) p. 170.